BOUNDARIES
&
PROTECTION

PIXIE LIGHTHORSE

Lighthorse Publishing, 2017
Redmond, OR

Library of Congress Control Number: 2017942264

ISBN: 978-0-9982953-4-3

Cover design: Joanna Price
Layout: Twozdai Hulse

Lighthorse Publishing
SouLodge Ranch, LLC
Redmond, OR 97756
www.pixielighthorse.com

BOUNDARIES

&

PROTECTION

HONORING SELF, HONORING OTHERS

"There is nothing more important for healers and wise people of all traditions than the creation and maintenance of good energetic boundaries so that we can live in balanced relationship to others and create a sustainable practice for ourselves. Pixie, as the great cosmic mother and wise woman she is, offers a dose of honest wisdom here - rooted in hallowed experience and served with a side of mellifluous love so that you feel seen, challenged, and held by this sweet medicine of a book."

– Athena Perrakis, Ph.D - Founder and CEO, Sage Goddess

"Reading Pixie's words, I felt like they had been strung together especially for me - a long string of lanterns, lighting my way toward wholeness."

– Christine Mason Miller, author of Moving Water: A Memoir

"Anyone struggling with saying no, dealing with trauma and addiction needs to be enlightened by her work."

– Jessica Stopera, Lead Program Facilitator at
Ramsey County Correctional Facility

"You will want to get a copy of this treasure trove of wisdom for EVERYONE you know and care about. It's that good, and that essential for maintaining healthy, loving relationships."

– Chris Zydel, Founder Of Creative Juices Arts

"Lighthorse's newest book will help you improve your relationships and experience deeper intimacy with others. These are important life lessons for we are social beings who need each other in order to survive."

– Jodi Crane, PhD, NCC, LPCC, RPT-S,
Counseling Professor And Play Therapist

"An illuminating book that shows in clear language how to create protective space. Lighthorse shows us that creating protective space doesn't have to be confusing or scary."

– Michelle Duncan-Wilson, founder of Soul Work For
Moms

*This book is dedicated to brave spirits
who pioneer new ideas in unexpected settings.*

To Jessica and Liz.

AUTHOR'S NOTE

This book is motivated by love and infused with magic—the magic that comes from understanding the profound laws of nature. My journey with boundaries practice has been companioned by my faithful spirit helper and queen, Mountain Lion. The book began as a three-time, best-selling e-course called Boundaries Boot Camp, which has helped many people put their relationships back on track.

Mountain Lion, North America's reigning species of big cat, is a spirit medicine helper who has been working inside of me for many years. I have found that her behavioral qualities inform my boundaries practice well. She moves fluidly, claims adequate rest, nurtures and teaches her young, is fiercely protective, territorial, graceful, walks softly on the earth, and is highly perceptive to sound and smell. Her golden color is like the rays of our creative sun, and as a transformational symbol, she embodies the masculine power of creating what we want. This is balanced with harmonized communication and adaptability. Though she is an apex predator, her medicine allows for receptivity and self-reflection. My first experiences with her were of tremendous fear, perhaps to be expected when we begin to interface with how powerful we are when we take responsibility for what we've been given.

My dream is that *Boundaries & Protection* will be a companion to those who carry it, and that its medicine will be integrated with application. I love people and believe in their ability to turn their lives around and hang in there when seas get stormy. I believe that if we bring intelligence in first through the spirit, then into the body, and lastly put it through the beautiful mind, we get a more miraculous response than if we reverse the order. Leading with the spirit seldom steers us down the wrong road. Leading with the mind leaves things to chance, because the mind has ideas that are governed by fear.

I began this book on steady ground. A good way through writing it, my legs began to quake—a typical reaction in the third stage of anything worth doing—when doubts creep in to see if they can undermine trust and confidence. I pressed on, knowing that the remedy is to follow my own damn advice: tune into your heart, call Spirit in to carry you, don't overthink it, and avoid negative gremlin-talk. It was a practice in leading with my spirit, which required the fears of my mind to take a backseat.

The contents of *Boundaries & Protection* are not the clinical opinions of an expert on the subject of human psychology and behavior, but of an experience, intuitive healer and teacher who loves people, life, and the gifts of Spirit as they express themselves in nature. My sacred time with thousands of women has been a robust teacher.

While reading, you may become aware of instances where you have violated someone's boundaries. Don't let it stop you from carrying on. Don't let it send you into a spiral of shame. You can make amends for mistakes and use this book to set things right again. The empowerment that comes from a boundaries practice lies in allowing mistakes and trusting that we have everything we need to make repairs.

This book is my offering to you of golden protection through your own murky territories where clarity is desired. It is intended to help you take responsibility for how your relationships are handled and enjoy the process of cultivating deep intimacy.

Pixie Lighthorse

CONTENTS

FOREWORD

Boundaries were once a perplexing puzzle to me. As I think back to the first half of my life, my lack of boundaries was often the source of my greatest heartbreaks, frustrations, and setbacks. In fact, this was true not only for me, but often for those I interacted with day-to-day.

I met Pixie after a particularly harrowing decade of personal tragedies and monumental mistakes. I've always been a big dreamer. Early on in life, I found ways to make amazing things happen—personally, professionally, and in relationships. It wasn't easy though, and there was often a whole lot of harmful fallout. After a toxic blowup with a friend that felt like it was going to break me once and for all, I sought out a teacher to help me navigate through it. Enter Pixie Lighthorse.

I had been struggling with boundaries for many years when I met Pixie. I knew I needed them, and so many things had happened that required them. I was simplifying my life by either letting people all the way in or closing them all the way out. This may be a step, but it is certainly not the destination. By the time Pixie and I had our first conversation, I was so exhausted by life that I was ready to close everyone all the way out.

Pixie introduced me to ideas and solutions that were so revolutionary to me, I can honestly say that I became a different person because of them. She spoke a language that was so clear, concise, fair, and honest that I felt great hope that I could someday reenter the world feeling safe from the hurt of others—and also that I could avoid hurting others, whether I was doing so consciously or not.

She coached me through some of the most difficult times of my life. I have always been left in awe and with great appreciation by the way she never takes sides, no matter how heinous something may look. She looks at everything objectively, with fairness, and with the intention of coming to a solution that satisfies all sides.

Over the years, Pixie and I have become very close friends. I watch the way she has navigated her own life, both personally and professionally, and my respect and love for her only grows. I've seen her moderate large groups of adults and facilitate squabbles among children. It is always a sight to behold, and I leave the experience wanting to do better. She has a natural sensibility that seems to have been born into her, but she has also traveled tough roads into her deep wisdom—and it is miles deep.

When I have my own interpersonal conundrums these days, I simply close my eyes and think about what Pixie would do. I know her well enough now to guess what she might do or say in certain situations. I almost always choose that route. When I don't know what to do, she is the first call I make.

Today I walk with a confidence that I have been envying in others for most of my life. I don't avoid difficult conversations anymore. I don't break out in hives when I have to be around people who used to trigger my every insecurity. I am able to speak my truth with fairness and love. I say no when I want to say no, and I say yes when I want to say yes. I am able to come to a place of forgiveness in just about any situation. I am completely okay if I am not a good match for someone. I don't take it personally anymore when someone else needs to have a more robust boundary with me. We are all humans trying to figure things out.

I have been begging Pixie for years to write this book, because I am constantly telling people that she has been my greatest teacher. It seems like everyone I run into in life is struggling to figure out how to assert fair boundaries. This book is an absolute treasure. I am certain that it will change your life experience as much as it has changed mine. Your relationships will blossom, your confidence will strengthen, and you will walk tall knowing that you are living and speaking your truth.

With deep appreciation,

Melody Ross
Founder, Brave Living

INTRODUCTION

What is a boundary? Why do we need protection? From what?

Boundaries are dividing lines between us and other creatures—in this application, humans. They denote where we end and someone else begins. Protection is an appropriate measure of safety from harm. We need protection because we humans harm each other, both accidentally and on purpose. We mishandle our emotions, which in turn affects other people's emotions. We say and do things to one another without thought to the consequences. Our attitudes have an impact on others and theirs on ours.

When we receive information about what is transmitting between us into our psychic systems and create beliefs out of them, we must be careful to discern what is true. Some untrue thoughts become beliefs that are life-altering, long-lasting, and deeply harmful to the spirit, which expresses itself through the body.

Practicing boundaries helps us know when to turn a thought into a belief and when it would not serve to do so. This is much easier to master as adults because our pre-frontal cortex isn't fully developed until we are 25 to 30 years old. Children do not know that they get to have boundaries, because parents act as their protection and serve as translators for which experiences are and are not okay. When children's boundaries are violated by caregivers, they internalize mixed messages about what is okay to say and do to another human. When we aren't sure how to treat and react to one another, relationships throughout our lives are difficult and painful.

We are living in disconnected times. It may seem that a call for boundaries and personal protection practices is a prompt to create more distance between people, by creating safety through shielding ourselves from unwanted experiences. This is only partly true and part of the work to be discovered. Too many limits feel like living in a cage.

Boundaries make room for the deeper connections and intimacy we actually want to have. As statistics climb about the incidence of chronic loneliness, isolation, and lack of belonging, it is not boundaries that are keeping people from one another. What keeps us from one another is fear of harm, which causes us to withdraw into our shells and away from one another out of fear of what will happen if we engage. This is primarily based on past experiences and an unwillingness to take risks for fear of feeling pain or reliving childhood suffering. We have become quite averse to feeling pain, because we have few skills that help us cope with it. Many of us avoid intimate relationships because we are seeking to keep the injured child inside of us as free from harm as possible.

The more secure we are that we can endure some painful feelings, the less we avoid one another. With an avoidant approach, we might have to feel something we don't want to, so we steer clear. If we set a boundary, we might have to talk about what helps us feel safe and stand up for ourselves. We might become vulnerable. We might experience intimacy, and if that gets taken away from us, it will hurt.

As our skin thickens with the means for coping, and we are able to move toward life rather than avoiding it, it is possible to find ourselves living with more vitality and less unbearable pain. Imagine that as the energetic space around you becomes hearty with firm flexibility, you will have more freedom to exist without fear of what terrible destiny could unfold. Boundaries make it possible for even the deepest feelers and highly sensitive empaths to be in the world enjoying copious amounts of rewarding intimacy.

When we're talking about intimacy with our loved ones, the kind that requires high levels of security and trust, we're essentially talking about how we must first come to trust in the process of life itself. If we cultivate a trusting relationship with Spirit or Source, then we are going to feel and see trust playing a big role on the stage of our life. If we prioritize creating peace in our overactive minds and endurance in our spirits, then we have a better chance of surviving the results of relationship—both positive and negative.

Humans want to feel secure, and if we look to people, jobs, food, health, money, and weather for security, then we will at some point have the rug pulled out from under us. With the very best of our abilities, we can try to maintain a sense of well-being through taking care of our basic needs for health and wellness.

When forces beyond our control unleash havoc on our lives, affecting what we perceive to be keeping us secure on Earth, our sense of inner security is compromised. It is guaranteed that unexpected events will happen many times throughout our lives, all the way until death. This we can be sure of. Grief and loss are real, and they are going to happen. The economy has and will again take a turn for the worse. People get sick. Tsunamis, hurricanes, and earthquakes are part of Earth's life cycle.

Another way to think about insecurity is as a fear of what could happen. It causes us to brace for the storms that are not actually happening right now. It is not true instability, but a preemptive emotional reaction to what we know is possible based on what has already happened. It is not our thoughts that cause us to act the fear out but the feelings that arise from those thoughts. The spirit has a way of wilting or soaring when it is moved by what the heart feels.

Respect is not only for humans to give to other humans. We can also respect the impermanence of life itself: the things we cannot control or maintain with any amount of effort, no matter how much security we think it will bring. What we can do is nurture attitudes of acceptance, while doing what we can to preserve the quality of our experiences. We can give to and of ourselves by looking at the greater system of life with awe. In this way, establishing healthy behaviors with other humans becomes a spiritual experience. It is how we give and receive without supporting unnecessary trepidation. Life itself is not a fixed and stable experience. Nothing we do will make it so.

Energetic and emotional territories are not bound by static, immovable fences or brick walls, keeping us from experiences that teach, fulfill, and shape us. New information, perspectives, and people help us to soften or firm those lines in the sand, as needed. Hopefully, this movement opens us rather than closes us down.

HOW TO USE THIS BOOK

Boundaries & Protection deals with what causes us to feel secure and insecure, and how knowing our limits can help strengthen our intimate relations. It provides an opportunity to zoom out and look at human nature more broadly than we can in our personal, daily experience of it in action—full of hurts and plenty of good reasons to avoid and resist depth and intimacy.

It should eventually inspire action leading to shifts and changes. The book breaks down what we say and how we act in ways that help new realities unfold.

As you read, your feelings will rise up. They are the driving force of our existence as humans. We may think our mind runs the show, but our powerful emotions direct us to act out the script.

The information contained here calls for the integration of how we think, feel, and act so we can take a more responsible role in how our relationships are turning out. It should also serve as support for modeling wiser ways for others, especially the children who are watching us closely to see what love and friendship looks like for big people.

After the first read-through, *Boundaries & Protection* will be a friend to council with when you're in a tight spot. It is designed to be shared with others, like bites from your coveted plate of nutritious fuel. I have tried to write each nibble with all parties of a relationship in mind—with compassion for what everyone on all sides undergoes when there is disharmony.

Some insights will help you know what's happening with your thinking and doing. Others are more aligned with your internal processes, the inward states where we are most intimate with ourselves, and where healing is done from the inside out. Above all, the small, digestible bites of content are meant to help guide you into your deeper realms of mature healing and wisdom.

Use the journal pages at the back to write down your thoughts and see how the process evolves over time. You may find that the book moves you in a circle, rather than from beginning to end in a straight line. It is not designed as an A-to-Z process that becomes complete. The beauty of life is that it moves in a spiral. My hope is that the words shapeshift for you as needed, coming across in the right way at the right time and supporting you from all sides.

Use this book in your classes, as part of your recovery protocols, and alongside complementary studies in growth and wellness. Have it near when you are working through conflict with loved ones. Dog-ear the pages that give your voice strength during difficulty. Let it be a source of support and comfort when you don't know how to handle a confrontation, and you want to run away. Stand your ground. Imagine Mountain Lion pacing a soft circle around you, illuminating your personal space, and reminding you that your energetic charge is felt by others.

Use this book to help you take responsibility for how you are experienced. Work with the language prompts to increase your courage and strengthen your boundaries. See if you can allow yourself to feel contained by visualizing her majestic presence.

GLOSSARY OF TERMS
AS THEY ARE USED IN THIS BOOK

Boundaries: lines that mark the limits of an area; dividing lines

Egg of light: a visualized protective membrane around an individual's electromagnetic energy field

Empath: a person tuned in to the emotional intricacies of a person, place, or animal

Empathy: the ability to share and understand the feelings of another

Golden bubble: see egg of light

Grace: courteous goodwill

Invasive: intruding on a person's thoughts or privacy

Limit: a point or level beyond which something does not, or may not, extend or pass

Projection: the transfer of one's ideas or emotions to another person; an idea of what is true for someone else

Protect: to keep from harm or damage with an appropriate measure

Source: any power greater than yourself that you turn to for comfort in your existence

Spirit: see Source

Stonewalling: refusal to communicate

Sympathy: sorrow for someone else's misfortune

Trigger: words, actions, events, or sensations that transport one back to an original trauma

Vulnerability: susceptibility to emotional, mental, sexual, spiritual, or physical harm

BOUNDARIES

&

PROTECTION

PIXIE LIGHTHORSE

START WITH SACRED

Let's say you're human with some loved ones around you, each riddled with fears and scars, joys and dreams, flaws and shadows. And let's say you feel disappointed with the way you're handling yourself in some of your relations with the people you love, and maybe you don't like the way you're being handled, either. Perhaps you're looking to improve your situation, so you can communicate without drama, reduce stress and frustration, or break old habits within your family.

Checking in with what is okay with you—what is fair and satisfactory and what is not—is a first step toward learning how a practice of boundaries can serve your life. By knowing what you want to ask of yourself and others, you can set the standard for how you'd like things to move forward. Relationships are the testing ground for our spirits to give and receive. The first thing to do is consider where you're at with the concept of sacredness: treating life as more than simply configurations of cells and atoms.

The questions that guide this work: Are you treating yourself and others as sacred? How about their treatment of you? What does sacred treatment look like?

These are big questions to consider, but they can be answered when we are clear about our expectations. Who doesn't want to feel sacred? Is there something preventing you from believing that you, others, and every living thing are sacred? How would you like to be treated?

Chances are that you're reading this book because someone else's behavior has crossed a line, and you'd like help understanding how to protect yourself or prevent further conflict. Or perhaps you don't yet have any obvious lines in the sand. Perhaps those you know are running willy-nilly all over your sacredness in an unwanted way and you feel powerless to change. Maybe you feel shame for violating the boundaries of someone you love and aren't sure how to mend it.

You're in the right place. Acknowledging sacredness is a solid place to begin.

PAUSE AND BUILD TRUST

Trust is nutrition for our souls and our relationships. Creating change inside of relationships, particularly fragile ones experiencing a high level of insecurity, requires time and patience. While it may be tempting to pick up the phone and tell so-and-so exactly how you will not tolerate their disrespectful and un-sacred treatment one more day, hold onto your emboldenment for a moment.

Allow the medicine of boundaries to work in your thoughts, your dreams, and your heart—even your digestive system (ever felt gut-punched by someone's hurtful words?). There is magic in absorbing a concept and implementing it slowly, maybe even with grace, so that you can become more sure of yourself. We don't want any heads to be lopped off in a sudden burst of boundaries over-assertion that you will later regret.

It can be quite a newsflash to find out that you are entitled to create a protective space around yourself and choose to be in unions that honor you. It can be equally challenging, but not impossible, to cultivate the level of self-respect that can support new choices for health and wellness.

For now, envision a golden bubble beginning to form around you. The challenge is that you must envision it around everyone else as well. Boundaries have to exist in all directions in order for them to work. It does not follow logic to ask others to respect your territory while you trample haphazardly through theirs.

I've found that when I decide to protect myself from the "stuff" of others, I am likewise held accountable to take an interest in protecting them from my projectiles. This requires a keen interest in knowing the parts I play in the matter.

Trust that you will become more clear with time and know what to do when the time comes to step into action.

CLEAN RELATIONS

What does clean relations mean? Think of the idea as having enjoyable relationships with those we love in which there are few resentments that are not being talked about. Clean relations are the ones you might describe as having a fair and equitable exchange of love and energy. Chances are, you can name several relationships you are currently participating in that are of a messier nature. Resentments are the natural result of not expressing unmet expectations. When held for too long, they cause internal conditions that I think of as ulcerations of the spirit.

It is not clean relations to hold grudges, gossip, cross-talk, stew, fester, hex, resent, cut and run without warning, quietly slip out the door hopefully unnoticed, ignore your desire to come clean, or refuse to admit the truth about what happened and what it was like for you. It is not clean relations to expect another person to do the checking in. It isn't clean relations to blame, shame, or project your idea of what someone else must have been thinking when they offended you. It is not clean relations to practice silent treatments, stonewalling, and invulnerability when you are hurt or angry.

It is clean relations to connect with someone because you care how they are feeling about what happened between the two of you. It is clean relations to check in with a loved one to ask if there is anything that can be done to soothe a stressful space after a disagreement. It is clean relations to let your friend know that what she said landed on a sensitive spot, how you are handling that, and what you might need from her. It is clean and fair to take the time you need to get your thoughts clear and allow others to do the same. It is fair to make clear that this is what you are doing before you step away, and bonus points for letting them know when you plan to return to the conversation.

The question is, do you value clean relations? Is it what you really want? What might happen to your current data if you upgrade your operating system to enable CR 2.0?

VULNERABILITY: GATEWAY TO INTIMACY

Once, I was asked by a therapist how vulnerable I was willing to be in a key relationship. I said I was willing to try, but I was quietly thinking, "Not very. Hmph!" When damage occurs by mutual dysfunction and resentments, one party lays the bricks, and the other spreads the mortar. Walls are built when we get to a point where we can no longer trust. We construct fortresses because we no longer trust how we will respond.

When intimate relations get ugly, we run for cover. Verbal abuse, physical assault, sexual mishandling, coercion, spiritual exploitation, mindscrewing, fearmongering, shaming, blaming, bullying, pressuring, silencing, interrupting, emotional neglect—all are reasons to implement boundaries. Some offenses call for releasing the relationship, as these hurts are unsustainable to fair, equitable, and clean relations.

For relationships that are not abusive, vulnerability is critical. Refusing to show someone how you really feel is denying connection to your real and true nature. Showing raw hurt can feel too risky, and a cloak of protective anger can help move some of the charge up and out of the body. However, anger is not the same as what lies beneath it. I think of it as the fire consuming the burning bush. It sends a strong signal, sometimes needed, but it also tends to eclipse other feelings.

When we are hardened as little children by trauma, it can be reflexive for us to begin to armor up in defense against even slight infractions—withholding our anger, tears, or acknowledgment of our confusion during a conflict, because we do not want to appear weak or fragile. It feels unbearable, and for children, it is. It is our first taste of powerlessness, and we don't like reliving it as adults.

Vulnerability is not a weakness. Our willingness to show up humble or in our feeling state is important for allowing our emotional components to be a part of our relationship, as they deserve to be. Just as our intellectual, spiritual, and physical aspects get to shine, so must our real feelings. When offered honestly, vulnerability is strength. It mustn't be used to manipulate, but as the inroad to healing conversations and paving the way for intimacy.

PROTECTING WHAT IS SACRED

Among the many things that are sacred—our fertile minds, our glowing spirits, our precious bodies, and our tender emotions—there is also our innocence. We do not live in a time or culture where people or children are considered sacred, holy, amazing, magnificent creatures. Past generational values paved our way here, but now we are saying that we want more. Sacredness was not a priority as it is now. We can celebrate by creating a whole new way. We can begin with one another.

At some point in our young lives, it was inevitable that our protective bubbles burst. Unfortunately, none of us had control over what stage of development that was. It is a shock to move from innocence to experience, and some occurrences leave deep scars. Even protective parents cannot prevent it happening to our children, try as we might. Life brings experiences, and some of them will shape us in ways that we will later want to re-sculpt.

Sacrifice of our innocence impacts the level of trust we experience as we continue on through life. Trauma causes us to wonder if we should brace for more of that kind of experience. Pattern trauma teaches us that we absolutely should. In order to avoid reliving that kind of experience, we seek to try on every adaptation we can, and yet, we sometimes find that we begin to draw what is familiar to us. How can we re-establish ourselves as sacred and learn new ways of being in relationship when what we know to do is so ingrained?

To make protection a value rather than a defense mechanism, find things you can protect to the very best of your ability—a garden, a plant, a child, an animal—and make a vow to be the guardian of something beautiful and keep it from harm. It is a good start for re-learning how to protect ourselves from harm. Combined with a willingness to act with self-respect and hold others in high regard, we can cultivate a sacred reverence for innocence and preciousness. Over time and with practice, you will see that you are sacred, precious, and beautiful, too. You will begin to expect better for yourself and better of yourself.

YOU ARE MAGNIFICENT

I will tell you so that you are clear: You are sacred. You are beautiful. You are magnificent.

You may need to make amends to another in order to feel strong about forgiving yourself for what you are holding onto. You may need to listen. Do what you must do. Clear the path for a new way of being. Stay in recovery. Call in the brass to help you with your health. Establish daily habits of exquisite self-care. They can be as simple as smiling at yourself and anyone you pass.

Think of boundaries as the sensation of having a golden bubble around the body. It is filled with our own radiant light. Vitality comes from life force, which is, quite simply, the frequency of the miracle of life. It is truly almost beyond comprehension that we exist in the way we do—with bodies that sense, hands that can give healing, language that can move our emotions, voices that carry sound, mouths to chew, wombs that gestate, and minds that create. We forget where we came from, how miraculous life is, and how it is growing and vibing all around us constantly.

It is your responsibility to step into your humble, courageous magnificence. We begin as impressive, exceptionally fine miracles, but we are taught to forget our miraculous nature. We are warned of the terrible danger of becoming self-centered and spoiled. We are told we're too-big-for-our-britches when we begin to show our strengths in early, undeveloped ways. The high price of these worn-out ethics is that we do not value ourselves as miracles. We will not value others as miracles, either.

When we know our magnificence and miraculousness, we can know others to be exactly the same. Everyone is splendorous. When a person acts from that place of radiant beauty, they stand out. The golden bubble is almost visible around them. When you step into what is golden about you—the essence of who you were before you were born—you will recognize it in others, too.

Vitality hums throughout a body that recognizes magnificence.

RE-BUILDING YOUR FOUNDATION

"But I don't have a foundation to rebuild. I've had the rug pulled out from under me since birth or longer. I don't have a home or a build-site, and no tools that I know how to use. I'm no builder."

Perhaps this is how you see it now. There can be times when we are at the end of our rope and hopelessness sets in. Our relationships are in shambles. We've reached a humble state of admitting that we may have had something to do with it. Shame, the lowest frequency of all and most lacking in vital life force, creeps in slowly and threatens to take over. Dark thoughts commence: "Who am I to deserve healthy relationships and love I can trust? I can't even trust myself. I probably deserve this."

We navigate our shadowy beliefs when we remember the pain of the past. When those beliefs dominate our thoughts, simmering woefully in the cauldron of the mind, we find that we have waded into the swamplands of the soul, upon which no structure can be built. We cannot establish a gritty foundation or build up resilience on bogs and quicksand. The sense is that we are slipping, can't attain mastery, can't get out of the hole...that we are destined to be prisoners because of where we came from.

The beauty of sinking into a mire is that it is precisely the place where a spiritual awakening is most likely to happen. Something about those dank, murky conditions are just fertile enough for Spirit's light to sprinkle through. The foundation for emotions needs a strong core, just as the trunks of our bodies do for walking, pivoting, bending, and flexing. We build that core like a pyramid beneath us. When we spiral up into the mind, where fear and old beliefs may lurk, the pyramid's broad base connects us to the Earth. It will help us stay grounded in the sturdy thinking that will get us through slippery states. For now, gently acknowledge that you can choose to say yes to wanting to be here on Earth and be well. You are gathering tools that will help with any quagmires that greet you down the road. Muster some courage and listen for what may be trying to come through.

WANT TO BE HERE

I think one of the greatest challenges to living on Earth is the lack of a genuine desire to be here. We have forgotten that it is our duty to be here (because we are here) and learn to be here in wellness. We have been given an undetermined amount of lifetime to do exactly that. Life itself is the quest, and too many of us think that we are not made for the journey, or that we are too fragile for the obstacle courses that present themselves. I believe that we are made to last, and that we are up to the task of finding out how to honor our lives as they came to be.

When I lead shamanic journeys, there is usually at least one student who, returning to Ordinary Reality with that in-between-worlds look, will dreamily confess that she didn't want to come back. I believe this means that something out there was so comforting, so exciting, so affirming, or so right, that it was tempting to stay. I prompt them to come back into and fully re-inhabit their bodies—look around the room at the objects that represent matter in this dimension, breathe and smile, and agree to be here again now.

Without a desire to be here, we don't have much to work with. The desire to be somewhere else is the phenomenon of craving that addicts report feeling beholden to, and it eventually sends them to their bottom. The altered state is more comfortable, uninhibited, detached, and emboldened. The unaltered state is perhaps anxious, shameful, disgusted, hopeless, hyper-sensitive, bone-tired, or seemingly broken beyond repair. Perhaps we think that in an altered state we have the ability to cope with the impossible obstacles. Unfortunately, the opposite usually becomes true. This is because not wanting to be here weakens our relationship to reality and to our spirits.

I think we are much stronger for living than we give ourselves credit for.

GROWING UP WITH ADDICTION

Addiction goes hand-in-hand with codependency, and what results is a life that isn't our own. In a codependent system, how we feel relies on how someone else feels. This is a structure that is, by design, set up to collapse. It is a locked pattern set on a loop. The loop may have a positive occurrence, but it will always swing down into a negative interaction cycle when addiction features are present. This is not because addicts, and those they have affected, were born negative or bad people, but because they are not yet able to take responsibility for their lives. Broken beliefs about themselves are still running the show. They haven't yet had, or haven't said yes to, their spiritual awakening.

It is possible that the pattern of the codependent system was imprinted on us at early stages of development. Addiction asks the child to bend herself into irregular, unnatural shapes in order to accommodate the caregiver's underdeveloped life skills. It is no accident that adult children of addiction report not knowing who they are. Coping skills for everyday life are slim to non-existent.

Growing up in an addict household means that the child's emotional and developmental needs are not met, and the golden features that naturally generate vitality are sent underground. Sometime around puberty, at the point when a person begins to see themselves in the reflection of others, the mind sets out on a path that can be doubting and mistrustful, establishing a high level of insecurity about simply being in the world. We cannot find where we "fit."

Part of boundaries practice can be declaring, "this insanity stops with me." Dedicate a good part of your energy to understanding the nature of how addiction plays out and repeats without a strong spirit to override the programming. We can heal our thoughts and our lives if we surround ourselves with wise people who have been through similar ordeals and come out the other side to tell a real success story.

PEOPLE PLEASING

People-pleasing occurs when we consciously or unconsciously alter our path in order to get a needed result from another, such as external validation or to avoid an unwanted outcome. Conflict-avoidant individuals often identify as people-pleasers, sometimes admitting it in a self-shaming way. How is it that we know we are behaving in a way that dishonors our lives and needs, yet continue doing it? Perhaps we haven't found another way yet.

An avoidant can thicken their skin by speaking the truth in very clear language. It might sound like, "I'm making a decision that's depleting me, and no one can help me but me. I can make a different choice."

If you made the time, how would you determine the terms of relationship? It is dysfunctional to commit "til death do us part." Our soaring divorce rate says that we need to make agreements that work.

What can become toxic for people pleasers is the silent resentment carried about their unacknowledged sacrifice. Unfortunately, those being "pleased" are not usually aware that their avoidant is harboring resentment, because they have never been told. When we chronically people-please, our lives do not belong to us. We are not honoring our lives by giving ourselves away for free, or for a silent price tag, which amounts to unmet expectations that were never agreed to.

A people-pleaser may become passive-aggressive when they decide to let their unexpressed resentments inform behavior and abandons the relationship without warning or explanation. "Passive" refers to being non-engaging on one's own behalf. "Aggressive" points to the energy that precipitates the leaving: silent blame and a punishing element. The person on the receiving end will have to "pay," though they will not have the opportunity to weigh in on the decision.

The key to repairing these situations lies in productive conversation: discussing how the pleaser has engaged in betrayal, and how to put things back on track. While new, this approach is totally possible.

LONE WANDERER

Most of us were not taught everything we needed to know about life: about exactly how to be a strong woman or man in the world, a parent, or a trusted friend. As generations unfold, each has a new set of standards for conduct, and this evolution seems to be changing even more rapidly today. What we have to work with are the models we grew up with, which, for better or worse, informs who we draw to us. Sometimes this begins as a comfort and can end up feeling like a curse. The mark of the Wanderer is that they perpetually seeks a destination without stopping to make a map.

Our brains become hardwired by what we are continually exposed to. Experiences train us to expect more of the same. They are reflected in the choices we make for ourselves in friends and partners.

This can leave even a very strong soul feeling adrift and orphaned, untrusting of life's processes, and unprepared for challenges. It is understandable on a beginner's journey to feel alone, without anyone who understands what it is really like. It's as if no one knows how to reflect our worth back at us, and we carry a broken mirror that projects a distorted image. We are happy to find someone who seems to understand. Sometimes it means that person was injured in similar ways, and this brings gifts and dilemmas.

The beautiful thing about wandering is that we are sure to come across hidden wisdom. There will be times when our theories will be disproven, and we will be surprised at what is revealed. Sometimes we take paths that have a high-ticket price. We pay with time, energy, and hard knocks.

At some point, we will want to make a change, and will go seeking with more enthusiasm for accepting what comes our way, sifting for the gems that will take us forward rather than leave us feeling like a victim of circumstance. We might be willing to take a risk in order to learn something new or retrieve something that we have forgotten.

Every Wanderer reaches a crossroads where they can choose to have more say in where they goes and what happens to them.

VISUALIZE THE EGG OF LIGHT

Soul work asks us to honor what's true, not what we've been programmed to believe is true. It finds us vulnerable and exposed to the elements. When we're in our healing process, our skin can feel thinner than when we are going about the usual business of life.

Engage your creative power of visualization. Imagine a semi-permeable membrane around your body that allows energy to flow in, but with just a bit of a pause before it reaches the part of your brain responsible for re-acting, responding, or freaking out: the limbic system. Seal yourself in a protective layer of high-frequency light. As information flows toward you, imagine yourself pressing a pause button, for just a second, while you run it through your filter. It may be rusty from underuse but will activate easier with applied effort. The key is to imagine yourself doing it, and that it is actually possible.

Think of the eggshell as an ambassador for your brain's executive function, your higher sense of reason, which allows you some distance between the information coming in and your emotional response to it. Your healing has helped you be less numb and more sensitive to subtle signs that will help illuminate your next action. Do you deflect what is coming at you, or do you allow it into your intimate space? Do you need more time to think about it? Try not to go into past trauma for instructions. Give yourself some time and space to consider what is informing your choice.

Using the Egg of Light visualization as a tool of awareness helps an individual feel secure in the higher knowledge of the choice to pause before responding. When we can see and feel protection in our mind's eye, it has an impact on our thinking, which has an impact on our being.

Many clients have exclaimed, "Egg of Light!" In a humorous way, this shows me that the client is aware of feeling exposed and that extra awareness allows for a sacred pause.

NAME IT TO TAME IT

Speaking and acting from the primal, fight-or-flight part of our brains can be wounding to precious relationships. The trouble is that damage caused in this state results in shame for the over-reactor. The need to repeatedly clean up what is or is not said in big fear and exaggerated anger is destructive to the soul of a relationship. When our primitive brains step up in fear, the best line of defense is a good offense: be prepared.

When feeling attacked, an individual will automatically defend in one way or another. Cognitive therapists recommend coming up with a name for what this feels like, in order to sense its pending arrival and have some say in what happens next. Defense doesn't always look combative or escapist. It can appear as shutting down, attempting to distract, changing the subject, or ignoring/denying the conflict. It is common to explode or shut down during this stage of conflict. Exploding may have different forms for you, such as hurling plates, yelling, or slamming doors. Imploding may mean that you initiate a toxic internal dialogue about why it's your fault, or a panic attack sets in. In all cases, the fearful body is primed for putting up its dukes or making tracks.

Taking responsibility for knowing what happens for you (and to you) in a given situation will help you know when to create boundaries around yourself, so that you can protect loved ones from your projectiles, as well as protect yourself from their verbal missiles. The Beast from Beyond, Limbic Lunacy, and Emotional Tornado are how I have described the phenomenon of my frontal cortex going offline and leaving me at the mercy of my monkey brain. Naming the oncoming sensation serves as a red flag for when my "lid" is about to flip, and all hope for a reasonable response is about to go to hell in a handbasket.

When we have some jurisdiction over our emotions, we are in charge of our lives. We can begin to take pride in how we conduct ourselves with others and take care of our emotional health. This is a skill that becomes more fluid with time and practice.

Learning to be responsible for how we contribute to dysfunction and managing our own "lids" is crucial.

BLIND SPOTS

In relationships, we leave our guards down when we're in a trusting state. We armor up when we're not. In non-abusive relationships—those that have routine conflicts without violence or oppression—individuals without healthy boundaries need more armor than those who have healthy boundaries. Just when things seem to be sailing along rather smoothly, an issue sprouts from an old hurt and triggers overwhelm and defensiveness. We say things that sting or throw something. Doors slam.

The dialogue kicks in: "Why didn't I know? What was I thinking when I allowed myself to be anything but suspicious and hyper-vigilant? How did I not see it coming? Surely this is a sign that my friendship is doomed and was probably cancerous from the start! What a fool I am!" The surprise of a boundary's violation can set off another looping internal pattern with no foreseeable end. I do not think any creature likes negative surprises, which is understandable.

One definition of a blind spot is "a loss of vision in a particular area," and they exist in the psyche just as they do to the periphery of the eye. They play out in relationships as the denial that something exists and needs addressing. We might see this as another form of avoidance of our part in the deal. When we choose to overlook or disregard, we will eventually be accountable for the consequence. A surprise wreck happens when we don't see, or worse, don't want to look.

We honor ourselves and others when we acknowledge and seek help for known issues during peacetime rather than under the threat of imminent war. It may take a little sleuthing to sort out what the actual matters are and what to do about them. Think of it as a humble act of loving care to scout out what is causing disharmony that may have been overlooked.

ESTABLISH GROUND RULES

It can be a good start to decide what you like and what you do not like to experience in relationship. In this vein, follow with what you think of as healthy behavior and unhealthy behavior. What would you like to see more or less of in each of your relationships? Would you like to see fewer silent treatments, less sulking, moratoriums on unconstructive complaining or staying out late without calling? Are you desirous of more communication, respect, identifying issues before they take you down, and clarity of expectations?

Determine some parameters for conflict. How we do conflict speaks volumes about the potential longevity of a love connection or friendship. In fact, how we do conflict determines the fundamental success of our relationship. Damaging, dysfunctional conflict wears a spirit down. It makes us tired and renders us hopeless. We reach our breaking point. In the beginning, we can tolerate much more than we will want to later. Once the fresh buzz of lovedust falls away, and our fantasy projections about the relationship and what it can do for us fades, we are left with the very real challenge of navigating the land mines of triggers and old, unresolved pain.

Avoid the three D's: demeaning, diminishing, and destroying. This will keep you out of trouble while you find your bearings, especially when your loved one agrees to share this value with you. What happens when someone violates the boundary? What is the consequence? What sounds fair, and what can you agree on? At what point do you seek mediation from a trained professional?

Make a habit of circling back, checking in, prioritizing vulnerable exchanges, and remembering what is sacred.

NO TRESPASSING

Think of a person with whom you have repeated conflict and boundaries violations. Get a picture of them in your mind. Now try to imagine letting them know that a specific behavior is no longer okay with you, and that you are establishing this rule to take care of yourself in a way you never have before.

Take a moment to feel into this boundary in a clean and clear way with fair language and a level-headed tone. You are in your full strength and grace. Power up the Egg of Light! What will happen if your declaration is received unfavorably? Do you have a plan that you can implement? Can you reframe your request in a way that will be more favorable to the outcome you're wanting to experience?

Imagine their reaction. Do you feel safe to set the boundary? Is it possible to ask for what you want? What will happen to you, or inside of you, if you do not? What might be possible if your request is well-received?

In some homes, a violation equals a hasty trip to the couple's counselor, mediator, or local sage for help. It is not a punishment, but a seeking of support when the violation is not a deal-breaker (cause for the end of the relationship).

At this stage, consider that you're painting the no trespassing sign. You haven't put it up yet—you're thinking through what it will be like to post it. As we explore the possibilities, we're activating our minds and entertaining what might happen. Consider what it will feel like when you make it known that you are interested in honoring their boundaries. Welcome them to share their thoughts with you about how you're coming across, offer feedback about what it's like for them, and share what they want you to know.

It may be that all parties want to hit reset and try again with newfound respect. This is when the magic starts to unfold.

EXAMINING EXPECTATIONS

In intimate relationship, we have much higher needs and expectations for fulfillment than we do with a co-worker or Great Aunt Edna. Many a marriage or friendship has fallen short of what is being wanted and effective language skills to communicate how to make the repairs are a mystery. What are your values in partnership with your children, siblings, and parents? What are your expectations for how you will be treated at work?

An inventory of our resentments usually lets us know where we're holding an expectation that we may not have admitted we have, that may be going unmet. Once you know the nature of how you do conflict with the people in your life, it becomes clearer how intimate you are with them. Understanding how you are inclined to handle conflict with the people in your life can clarify why you are more or less intimate with one or another. What hurts inside of these relations, and how are these hurts handled?

While you are in the early stages of observing how you do relationship, (the thinking stage, which is the precursor to acting and the deeply connective force that is feeling), you are in a powerful position to hypothesize about the matters of relationships without getting emotionally fired up to the point of overwhelm and jumping ship before you try something new.

Emotions drive our passionate life—the life that generates more chi and juice for vitality. Taking the opportunity to observe with objectivity is not about numbing the feelings out and making choices from intellect alone. It is simply the first step in taking a here-and-now snapshot of how we've come to be in this position of needing to walk with protection. It is fascinating to me that as I've become clearer about why I need boundaries, I have had to exert less effort to keep them in place.

With due amounts of self-respect, we don't have to think about it so much.

CONTRACTS

People are not business partners, except for sometimes when they are. However, even at work, we're emotionally affected by the internal systems of others. Anyone can become triggered, overwhelmed, abandoning, or avoidant. However, when it occurs with someone we closely love, we tend to unload the full measure of our piled-up thoughts and emotions on them more readily.

At work, it might be someone from Human Resources who handles the "humanness," and what it entails. In our home relationships, we do not have such a department for mediating interpersonal conflict. It is up to us to make terms of agreements that go beyond "'til death do us part" and infant/parent bonds. While we don't want to parent our significant others, it seems common that one partner is usually driving the improvements bus, while the other either rides along or tries to jump off as their emotions direct them to.

Making mutual agreements and decisions about the relationship and how it's turning out may seem like micromanaging. But as time passes and unresolved issues grow more intimidating, inattentiveness sets in. Date nights, connective in their fun-loving way, have made a comeback. Couples are taking the time to enjoy each other. More formal sit-downs to check-in with lingering feelings and topics of concern can be scheduled, too. Time together is well-worth the investment. Making monthly or as-needed dates to check-in designates time to resolve any lingering issues.

It can be very comforting amidst life's bustle to know that our family makes time to sit down together, share what's on our hearts, and re-bond after time away, physically or due to mental preoccupation. I can tell when my people need to get close and remember that we love and trust one another. If the chief question between two people in relationship is "Are you there," then it goes without saying that check-ins, re-bonding time, and feedback will be beneficial.

TRYING ON NEW WAYS

Approaching a partner, friend, or child may pose some challenges when you try to communicate in a new way or march in with your clipboard and declare that things are gonna change. Old dogs, especially parents, in my experience, do not welcome a new set of rules after decades of their way working "just fine." It may be that you are not able to overhaul anyone's systems but your own.

Take heart; the relationship can still work. Many programs, including those designed to help people recover from addiction, do not rely on members of the family to enthusiastically jump on the sobriety bandwagon with them in order to work, thankfully. What it does require is that we make room for one another to turn over new leaves and bring the wisdom back home to the relationship hearth without admonishment and being impatient for results.

This is where it is important to recognize that our timing may not be our loved ones' timing. Nevertheless, one foot forward in the right direction can save a life, marriage, or bond. It only takes one person's shift to create a new ripple.

As you work through your thoughts about what you would like to become more solid in your home tribe and friendships, you will know with whom you can test new strategies and exchange feedback. It may happen that you are able to consult with your significant other about how to interact more responsibly with a child or parent, bringing him or her on board for the process without overwhelm. Later, with new language gathering between you, and by showing that you have a keen interest in handling all of your loved ones with integrity, it may be easier to have needed conversations at base camp.

If you can set boundaries at work (no more weekends, no more twelve-hour days), it will be a model to those around you, who will hopefully cheer on your decision to take better care of yourself. This outside-in approach will also help you learn more about who you are when you are treating yourself with greater respect.

HEROIC JOURNEY

Why do we seek to improve our situations? Why can't we be happy with the way things are? I think we can be, while considering that the human spirit is naturally driven to connect to life that grows and changes, sprouts and releases, dies and composts.

Building walls, avoiding conflict, people-pleasing, overreacting, and inciting drama, prevent connection. This does not create more trust with loved ones. We use these tactics to get the love and connection we seek, but there are more effective ways. When the past or broken modes of thinking determine how we relate, we feel the charge of an emotional connection, but not in a way that creates more secure experiences.

Transpersonal and Jungian psychologists maintain that there are many stages of development, each preparing us for becoming a hero. A hero is defined as one who comes through the challenges of life and is made stronger by them. In a sense, that would be all of us, or could be at any time, should we recognize it. Maintaining lasting and trusting relationships is an act of heroism.

The hero's journey follows developmental stages from adolescence to maturity. The grooves created in childhood determine how we will move through the stages. Our developed levels of courage and resilience, grit, and perseverance, and whether we had support will have an impact on what we can endure. Some get to a stage they cannot seem to grow past. The adventurer comes to a place where they've done some healing, gathered some tools, warriored for a cause, and is ready to share what was learned. It may look like showing someone an unforgettable kindness, uplifting others with gifts of song and food, being of service in your community, or mentoring youth going through what you did.

Believing in others is a clue that we're on an altruistic path. It's a signal that we've gained wisdom and feel confident to pass it along and pay it forward.

IDENTIFYING THE DESIRED OUTCOME

What can one expect when relationships are reorganized for health and intimacy? We may be able to get the love we're yearning for by understanding our part in the deal. Before listing the exact criteria you'd most enjoy in a friend or significant other, think about what's feasible and your deal-breakers.

We seem to go through relationship wanting our partners to be our everything, to complete us, to know us better than we know ourselves. This is a tall order and unlikely to be delivered. It may be enough that we offer one another empathy and enjoy the companionship.

We may want our parents to see and acknowledge our accomplishments, our glowing magnificence. It may be enough that they honor our limits for hearing criticism and stop parenting us into our thirties and beyond.

We may want our children to listen closely and follow every instruction we give them, which is impossible (and growing more so as external stimuli increase and our attention becomes more divided). I'll settle for a nightly deep-dive snuggle and check-in, rather than hold them to unmeetable expectations during daylight hours for which I hold a nightlong grudge. For older children, it may be enough to honor limits while in your home and do not violate financial or educational agreements.

Deal-breakers can and should include no violence and no substance abuse. Limits could include no name-calling, no condescending, no arrogant superiority trips/power tripping, no disappearing for hours during or after a conflict without at least a briefly stated plan for returning to resolve the issue. These are reasonable items to ask for and offer to our loved ones.

The outcome we're hoping for might be more simply stated, to be resolution-oriented, allow my friend to freak out because of something I do or say, be allowed to do the same, honor myself, learn to communicate my feelings by sitting with them before I speak, claim space to heal, cultivate security by trusting my intuition, not indulging my fear, and know and honor which actions are self-respecting and which are not.

MAKING WAVES

What kind of waves do you want to make on Earth? Every day, the weight of our footprints, our intentions, and the results of those intentions create an impact that ripples out to others.

If you could see how a doe puts her hoof on the ground, you would know why she and her kind live, though she is the favorite food of many predators. If you could see how the velvet paw of the mountain lion moves through the desert sand, you would know why she seldom goes hungry. Deer and lions don't move softly because they are in perpetual fear or always stalking. They move softly because it is their nature to do so. They also jump, play, and run, all in the way that their divine essence dictates.

When we're clear about how we want to move through the world, we change the culture. We make repairs by envisioning the impact we want to have, trying out new methods, seeing what the results are, and adjusting when needed. We have become addicted to asserting our existence with a dramatic and desperate show to be seen, heard, and understood.

Boundaries work addresses issues caused by chronic misunderstandings about which behaviors are okay in relationship and on the earth. Those who make an effort to honor themselves and honor others help the collective population shift. We make the effort to cultivate good love and clear communication to generate vital life sparks and come to relationship bearing the energy of HOPE.

Imagine that you are protected at all times by your consciousness and willingness to feel what comes up to be felt. Imagine that your sacred pause, and eggshell buffer is engaged and ready to determine what is coming at you that needs some dealing with. Uncover new possibilities for being with people rather than avoiding them—many kinds of people!

Awareness is everything. Envision yourself moving with your divine flow and follow that energy, not in the clunky ways of your programmed trauma.

CHOOSE YOUR ARMOR

Utilize the metaphor of armor to visualize that there is a barrier between you and pain coming toward you in the form of verbal darts, resentful arrows, bullets of disappointment, poisonous glares, and clubs of projection. Now imagine that the most effective armor of all is the unwavering belief that you will be okay. If you are not in true danger, begin with knowing that you can withstand another hurricane of big feelings and that you will get through. Trust that you are learning how to be inside conflict and manage your responses for a better outcome.

If you have chosen to be in relationships where conflict often leads to war, it's likely that you have been weathering the storms for some time and have built up some resilience. Yet it can still be surprising how fear of not being able to survive another disruption acts as fuel on the flames of dispute, even with our dearest co-conspirators. Helpful armor could be a few deep breaths, techniques to resolve anxiety in the moment, a cap of creative problem-solving, willingness to listen, and the humility to own your part. A passive role counts as a part.

If you are in relationship where the injuries come from silence or neglect, have you found ways to inhabit the awkward space until resolution can be had, or is more damage done in the introversions of the mind? Either way, moving toward resolution and easing out of habits that find you shutting down can help immensely.

There is a middle road to be found between waving your sword, taking prisoners, and locking yourself in the dungeon.

CHOOSE YOUR WEAPON

Let it be language. Support words that truthfully represent your experience are your ally. The more you can describe what it's like for you, the more understanding you are liable to get. It's okay if words are not your area of expertise. It doesn't take very many words to communicate where in the conversation you felt confused, hurt, sad, or angry. Keep it simple.

Let it be considerate timing. Bedtime may not yield the desired results for conflict resolution, as bed serves well as a space for sacredness and intimacy, snuggles, and pillow talk—a safe and neutral space where couples and families go to sleep peacefully, having resolved disagreements out in the commons. It's okay to table a conversation if talking about it now will leave you exhausted tomorrow. Maybe all parties make a date a few days from now and take some time to write down their thoughts. Conditions may not be right for resolution. Think about what would change that.

Let it be a talking stick. A favorite tool is a beautiful stone or stick to pass around among disgruntled family members. During conflict, someone here is often dashing around looking for it, desperate to be heard. The holder empties out thoughts and feelings while abiding by the terms (no demeaning, diminishing, destroying, condescending, name-calling, touching, power tripping, projecting, shaming, etc.).

Let it be you who leads. "I" statements help move the process along, so that the speaker isn't further triggering the dedicated listener with accusations and projections about all of the things they did wrong.

Let it be a professional. Living with dysfunction is not a noble pursuit. Call in a therapist when consult is needed. When I was growing up, I was often triangulated in my parents' disputes (a boundaries violation in itself). Later, I suggested they go to therapy. I hadn't made it clear that I wanted out of their dysfunctional tennis game. I was told that therapy was an admission of failure that showed you weren't able to take care of your own issues. This left me scratching my head in confusion, though it did shed light on how previous generations tolerate what subsequent generations are unwilling to.

WHEN TO WALK AWAY

Wouldn't it be ideal if quarreling meant fighting for a relationship's integrity and security? Fighting is often about one or more parties trying to be right, with an element of "hear me," "see me," or "appreciate me" present. It is understandable, particularly when there are elements being unmet on a regular basis. That being said, a push to have an intense conversation in a hostile or unwelcoming climate seldom yields desired results.

Engaging in inflamed words and behaviors with frequency has a tendency to damage trust between people and wear down their hope. Even when we choose not to take the words and actions of others personally, fighting overstimulates our adrenals, depletes our emotional reserves, and does little to reinforce the vitality of the bond. Every once in a while, an agitated rearing up can be a reminder of the fire and passion contained for each other, and the relationship is worth fighting for. If words are being slung that come back to haunt, you might consider the value of the exchanges and the impact they have—not just on those sparring, but on little ears and bystanders who often don't know how to process extreme levels of stressed emotions.

Walking away, in its light aspect, is a responsible decision, especially when things turn hot and unproductive. Table a volatile conversation until the timing is right and favorable conditions can be created for resolution. Allow parties to collect their thoughts in order to respond with more care and responsibility. Tend to that flared-up limbic system, which signals you to step back and breathe your frontal cortex back into place before you say or do something you regret.

Walking away in its shadow aspect is to ignore the issue, discount the feelings of the other, blow off, and disavow one's part. Denying that you have a responsibility to the emotional health of the relationship is a serious matter, so this is one to think over before you find yourself heading for the exit as a means to diffuse a skirmish.

FAIR FIGHTING

If you find fighting to be a zesty enterprise among consenting adults, you might find that you and your significant other or family members are proficient at hashing out the feels while respecting boundaries and sensitive areas. Fair fighting seems to be much more possible among trusting intimates than casual acquaintances and co-workers.

Little ears may not understand your ways, so be mindful of what is being modeled for the young ones. Though they may be conditioned to witness it by example, their ability to compute sarcasm and some adult expressions doesn't develop until the pre-teen or teen years. Certain figures of speech and vocabulary will be over their heads, so consider the impact of your more impassioned melees. You might ask them how they feel when arguments take place. Fair conflicts that come to loving resolution are an excellent way to show them how it is done. Make at least part of your amends in their presence so they can witness the completion of a process and go back to not worrying about you.

Fighting to some may sound like debating to others. Lines can be crossed when someone wanders casually over the hedgerow and pokes on a tender spot, which in turn inflames the other. If this is done maliciously, it can hurt.

There are ways to move through an issue with care and respect for the other. It requires being able to self-reflect inside of the argument. My partner and I can be heard saying things like, "You're right about that part," "Fair enough," and "Okay, I'll take a look at that," right in the middle of a passionate debate, though difficult at times! This is when conditions are well-suited, and we can stay in the conversation. It is definitely a learned skill that takes practice. However, once someone flips their lid and becomes governed by fear, suspicion, mistrust, resentment, or possession by the ego, these awesome strategies fly right out the window.

Learning to fight fair is well worth the effort, especially for self-identified hotheads, Scotch-Italians, and soccer fans. If you forgive easily and move on quickly, you are good at this one.

EGO STRENGTH

Being able to hear feedback is a sign of ego strength. Our ego is not a function to be resented, killed, or amputated. It is responsible for helping us show up in the world and get from point-to-point and is a critical aspect of the working psyche. Without ego strength, we are like a tall tree planted in shallow ground: unable to withstand the rigors of relationship when it's time for us to be held accountable. A strong, humble ego is like a deeply rooted willow, reaching deep for underground water, able to bend and flex in the wind.

Cultivating ego strength is making an effort to become fortified with confidence, willingness to listen, forego inflated features of self-importance, and soften over-reactive responses. It means we have a healthy sense of humor and get offended less easily, and do not use being offended as a weapon against our loved ones.

Going out into the world with our egos intact is much more useful than taking to the streets with no ego. It is a checkpoint that registers incoming information and reacts with a fitting response, not a mask to avoid appearing vulnerable or concerned with what others will think.

Ego strength helps us manage ourselves inside of relationship by relieving us of all of the blame or all of the righteousness. It recognizes that there is a middle ground, a moderate path. You can recognize it in conversation because it seldom shows up as defensiveness or uses absolutes like "always" and "never." It leans back, folds its arms over its chest and says, "Hmmm. I hear you, and I'll take that in and verify whether it is true." It is curious and willing to explore new concepts and possibilities where there may be unseen errors.

The trademark of ego strength is it enables us to hear feedback without crumbling.

It is one of the most crucial elements of enforcing boundaries without building walls. It requires that you love the truth more than you love being right, and you are willing to seek it out.

COMPASSION FOR ANXIETY

The word "fight" raises hairs on the necks of most because there is a charge to it. It doesn't literally mean combat, but it can feel that way to some. There is an art to doing it well and in a way you can be proud of. A well-played fracas can help a relationship feel more successful than sweeping feelings under the rug in order to keep the peace at all costs. For those who find any sign of a disturbance anxiety-producing, extra care is needed, while leaving room for a range of emotions to be present in a conflict.

Have a plan for what to do when hostilities flare to the point of an anxious spinout—with the potential for more to come. A solid plan includes code words and exit strategies, which are particularly helpful for folks who have PTS, anxiety, and panic attacks. I have been known to stop an argument to go and stand on my head to get my blood flowing, as some types of fighting seem to freeze up the circulation of oxygen to my brain! No loving partner wants to see their sweetheart breathing into a paper bag or reaching for pharmaceuticals while they're making a genuine effort to be present to what ultimately can cause a lot of internal stress.

Watch for your loved one's signs of overwhelm and collaborate with them to make a decision to resolve the issue later. This loving act of kindness is boundaries and protection at its best and goes a long way toward maintaining trust.

If you are close to someone with an anxiety condition, know that it is real. It can feel incapacitating for them to move through what seems effortless for others. A person with an anxiety condition might make great strains to show up at the negotiation table but may need to write down their thoughts and take time to become clear about their emotions and how to convey them. They may need more time than seems reasonable for choosing a response. They may not be able to be as spontaneous in conflict as you'd like them to be. Try to be patient and love them anyway.

FANNING THE FLAMES

We know what naughty tricks to pull out when we feel threatened or want to yank someone's chain. What motivates this behavior could be insecurity, immaturity, a desire to confuse and redirect the conversation for personal gain, or an unwillingness to stay on course with a goal of resolution in mind. When instigating shows up, it's anyone's guess as to what's behind it. What results is a tendency to get stuck in familiar circular patterns that lead nowhere. Many a bad argument with no legs to stand on can be attributed to someone dedicated to trying to get a rise out of their opponent for fun or to serve the ego.

Fanning the flames of conflict can also be a diversion tactic for getting the other person to act out in a way for which they can be ensnared and blamed. The instigator needs to know that this is not an enjoyable game. Depending on the person and the perceived value of the relationship, it may fall on deaf ears. When we can identify that we're acting this way, sometimes that's all it takes to inspire a change.

If we feel manipulated when we're making a genuine effort to be resolution-oriented, a vigorous burst of hot air can set a wildfire raging across the hills and burn what could be a productive conversation out. This becomes arguing to argue. Unless you majored in debate and know the rules of making solid arguments, no good will likely come of it. The relationship stands little chance of coming out undamaged when mean-spirited banter persists. Teasing in order to get a rise out of someone feels exploitative, and it can be challenging to recover from these kinds of violations.

Undermining a healthy process is not what most of us want in our primary relationships, so you might recognize this as a phenomenon that turns up at work or in settings other than home. If you've inadvertently stoked someone's defenses, course-correct, restore trust and safety, and find a more respectful way to communicate.

COURSE CORRECT

When communications head for quicksand, pull things back on the good road. It may be entirely up to you to do this for your relationship, and you may resent this fact. Decide what is most important: to initiate resolution in order to restore peace and harmony, or to wait expectantly for your loved one to steer your relationship in the right direction when they have shown you this is not what they can do. They may be very willing to partner, even if leading isn't their strength.

Some boundaries work is about taking the initiative and modeling the behaviors you want to encourage. It may feel like a solo enterprise, but the alternative is that no one sets the bar and paves a new way. When the spark of descent into unhelpful territory threatens to ignite, take a breath. Take the time you need and get that ship sailing straight with clear language and realistic expectations for where it can go right now. It may be that you get as far as you can today and attempt a new level tomorrow.

It is okay to make mistakes. We can take back things that came across harshly or unfairly. We can forgive others and ourselves for veering off-path. It happens. It is a sign of emotional intelligence to clean up errors and move on. While we cannot unfeel the pinch of a stinging string of words or careless deed, we need not carry grudges for minor infractions that have been apologized for. In relationship, unreleased grievances pile up and lurk in wait. The habit of not letting go of what is no longer relevant can haunt a relationship with good bones and disable it over time, slowly and painfully.

A humble and sincere, "Oops. I'm sorry," should do the trick. If it is not enough to set you back on track, check-in to see if there is more that can be unearthed and addressed. If not, keep it simple.

OVERSTIMULATION

In a state of anxiety, the sufferer is in fear and pain. Chemicals in the brain are lagging and surging, and the body's system is out of balance. Boundaries for the overstimulated include stepping back from conflict and reclaiming the breath. This could take minutes or hours. The following are a few words that have been medicinal for those in my tribe. They are supportive, affirming that everything will be okay.

I am not alone. It is safe to feel my real feelings, seek others in my position for support, and admit the nature and origin of what is happening now. Healing occurs over time. I can be patient and check-in with my soul while making healthy choices on my own behalf. While I am in my healing process, I can be open to life.

I can find fair language that helps me to be responsible for my health and wellness. I can express from my own heart without blaming and making another wrong. I will know what to say and do once I've become clear about what is true.

I have a hand in how things unfold. I can make a choice to be humble and allow healing. My voice is my own, and what happens from here is up to me. I may think something is terribly unfair. What can I do to bring things into balance?

I only need to be me. I do this well when I am connected to the Source that fuels me. I can name that Source in my way and find all of the ways that facilitate the recharge I need. When I am enough for me, everything shifts, including how I experience scarcity or abundance, love or rejection.

What can help me be more at ease and in charge of my life and feelings? I needn't numb out the discomfort, but instead seek to understand what my existence is about and how I operate.

STEPPING BACK FOR CLARITY

When the heart rate hits one hundred beats per minute, it's time to step back. How long might it take before you can become resolution-oriented? Are you honoring what your body is telling you? What do you need in order to find yourself open and willing at the negotiation table?

For those in partnership with people who experience an increased heart rate that elevates with conflict, it's time to be sensitive and learn all you can. Patience and compassion help us understand why spontaneous boundaries are being set sooner than we might expect or need. Those with childhood trauma and compromised coping mechanisms may lack the bandwidth for that pressing decision or conversation you would very much like to have right now.

Asking them to behave like you or "like a normal person" is simply unfair, because their body's stress response is firing before yours does. In a more extroverted person, or someone very eager to perform under pressure, they may be moved quickly to anger, agitation, or frustration. Sometimes this is because they are managing several conversations at once inside. More introverted types, who process internally, may be seen shutting down or appear overwhelmed.

Whether it is you or the person you are trying to communicate with, stepping back is a gesture of love. The key is to notice the symptoms, honor them, and make a time to circle back to the conversation when the surprise factor has settled. To claim some space to become clear is to make an offering to the soul of the relationship. A thoughtful and cooperative hiatus, in which time and energy are given to recovering the valuable aspects, is generous and wise.

Though it may not seem to be the best decision for us, it may be the best move when one or more parties is simply unable to get to where they need to be to stay active in the conversation.

KNOW YOUR LIMITS

Certain behaviors seem to be universally undesirable, but you may have limits you can honor in a way that are very specific to you. The term "stalker" has become a household word and refers to someone who is obsessive or fixated on being in relationship with us. It's something we typically don't want to experience. When you feel flanked by a person whose motives do not seem in your best interest, your red flags may go up slowly or right away. With practice and awareness, one can intuitively perceive unsafe behavior before it becomes an issue. We can set ourselves up for success by knowing what feels safe for us today.

While you are in the early stages of sobriety (or ever within your sobriety), maybe it happens that you cannot be in relationship with people who use drugs or alcohol at all. Perhaps you know that you are not able to have successful friendships with those who exhibit borderline personality disorder, bipolar disorder, or manic depression while you're healing your parent wound. You get to make the rules. It may benefit you to consider that they may not be forever rules, but they currently need to be enforced. Maybe, beyond what you're going through now, the road will change course and something else will be possible.

Perhaps you need twenty-four hours or more to make critical decisions that will affect the trajectory of your family's life. Maybe you need time alone to collect your thoughts after a skirmish. Maybe text-arguing is fruitless, and you require face-to-face or voice-to-voice communications with resonance. It's not too much to ask when you know what works—it is responsible and wise.

Rigid rules are not easeful on relationship, so with partners or close loved ones, consider declaring a few meaningful limits rather than a laundry list. They will be easier to remember and honor, and you will respect yourself for knowing what you need and asking for what you want.

MENDING AND BENDING

What doesn't bend will break. Boundaries are not fixed walls of stone. A broken trust can sometimes be mended with time and consideration. Remember to ask yourself what it will take to allow someone back into your orbit. If you don't know right away, it's okay. But circle back from time-to-time and truthfully check-in with yourself.

A willingness to name our part in a disagreement may find us initiating contact and inviting someone back into our lives from whom we have taken a break. Reaching out after time apart can happen when there has been time for self-reflection and realization of the value of the relationship. Coming back to a relationship wiser, stronger, and more willing to take responsibility for what we are feeling and wanting can be pretty exhilarating. It can help us know what kind of friend we are and can be.

I have had friendships that became challenging to manage. There are times in our lives when we are not as available for one another as we want to be. Two lives under stress can put a friendship to the test. Working through the difficulties has led to some beautiful experiences and reunions. Hurt feelings needed time for review. Expectation-informed resentments required fair examination. Egos benefited from humbling and strengthening. Fears needed to be calmed.

What helps immensely is to act with integrity by avoiding cross-talk, to hold one another in high regard despite differences, to honor the beauty of the relationship and good times shared, and to tend to one's own part in the original dissolution.

COOL OFF

Once we've become inflamed, we can protect ourselves and others by quickly prioritizing a cool-down period. Many a boundary has been violated when a flared-up individual decides to ride that pony all the way to the finish line. While there is nothing wrong with anger, those who express it in large quantities and often, may need to ask if they're being lazy about how they're expressing it. Those who are not expressing it may need to ask what is underneath the holding back.

When internal temperatures have caused damage in your relationships, it's important to find new ways to protect your health and heart by taking responsibility for the state you're in. Perhaps more importantly, you will need to protect those around you. Stay in your bubble, and do not unleash your anger where it will cause more damage, especially to fragile systems you are in the process of repairing.

Make agreements with the people around you about how you express yourself when angry. It may be that certain levels of impassioned expression are totally acceptable. When you do not make agreements, there will be clean-up to do.

How do you feel about anger? Are you accepting and acknowledging of your own? The more at ease we are with our own expression of red-hot feelings, the more we may provide room for others to do the same. But comfort levels with anger should not be the determining factor for setting a limit. It can be uncomfortable. When we get right down to it, it's a necessary part of our catalog of emotions. Anger expressed in a healthy way can be a great healer. In some disputes among the equal-tempered, energy is matched on either side during a disagreement and hopefully both sides can be heard and empathized with.

Navigating anger with care is a must if you want to practice boundaries like a pro. I'm always impressed to hear the truth in its simplest form: "I'm angry." When followed by, "I'm going to take a walk and get a handle on it," I'm dazzled. When we're too angry to communicate the way we want to, a cool-off period can help.

EXPLAIN YOUR STRATEGY

When handling your emotions and responding to another's, it is excellent practice to verbalize your plan for moving it to a solution and naming the results you desire. If you know that you need to take a long break from a relationship, be honest with the other person. Make a promise to revisit the matter in a specified amount of time and follow through on it. In difficult-to-resolve dilemmas, it may be helpful to ask how you can be supportive to the relationship while taking the time and space you need to become clearer.

If you're healing a trauma, come up with a preliminary plan you can stick to that demonstrates your willingness to handle your part with care. Become clear about what is expected of you and whether you can meet it. Explain what you expect from the other and remember to set a date to circle back and check-in to maintain connection.

In short disagreements, a strategy that seems to work well under pressure is to stop talking about the content of what happened that caused the situation and focus on how you need to handle what is coming up for you. Give the other the chance to do the same. It may be that a pattern showing up which is causing fear or a breech in trust which is higher priority.

For bigger deals, which require more time, patience, care, and consideration, map out a path to how you see the relationship getting to where you want it to go. See if you can agree to a reasonable arrangement. If a boundaries violation has occurred, what needs to happen to get back on track? If you haven't had any boundaries in place, and need to declare them, let the party involved know that you are working to have healthier relationships and need to gain a clearer understanding of where you didn't honor yourself.

In close, intimate relationship, it even helps to state that you need to make a call to a trusted friend or advisor who is an advocate for you both, and you'll return to them shortly.

TIME OUT FOR RAGE

Rage is a natural and understandable result of trauma by another person or an injury. Accident-related trauma can produce a level of confusion that intensely frustrates the injured and may cause them to unleash on bystanders.

When childhood trauma is pressed into the subconscious because it has not had a safe place to be expressed, it becomes more volatile and harmful to the person carrying it and those who experience it "leaking out" in unexpected ways. Rage can become triggered easily by circumstances that bear even a remote resemblance to the original traumas.

When a rage attack comes on, an immediate time-out can press pause on the process. The person feeling the surge of emotion must handle their rage responsibly or face the consequences of damage and the breakdown of trust that results from misdirecting it. It is important to disengage, work through the stressful emotions in a healthy way that considers the bystanders, and honor what is inside the body causing the reaction.

A time-out allows the executive function of the brain to come back online after what can feel like an intense electrical surge. Acknowledging the perceived threat to one's stability for what it really is—in most cases, a trigger into the past—can help spare those in front of you from paying the price for the trauma behind you.

No amount of blame on another person can justify raging on them, but the narrative of unresolved trauma will make a mighty effort to convince you otherwise. No mistake deserves a rageful overreaction. Raging directly on a loved one will always damage the relationship in some capacity, in the form of fear to the recipient and shame for the person who lost control of their emotions. Being in relationship with someone who rages can cause one to question whether they should have stronger boundaries or if misdirected rage is a deal-breaker. Calling a time-out is a way to begin.

UNDERSTANDING RAGE

When a person's anger turns to rage, it is likely that the primal part of the brain, the limbic system, has become overstimulated to the point that it has taken over the conversation. When someone "flips their lid," the executive function of the brain responsible for higher reasoning has stopped working temporarily. Fear, big emotions, and maybe confusion and chaos are reigning. For people with traumatic brain injury (TBI), this may happen more frequently than in others. Head trauma can affect development and function of the frontal cortex. It has also been found that concussions can be responsible for interference with communication. Commonly referred to as "fight-or-flight" or "monkey brain," the instinctual function is alarmed into an overblown emotional response.

Setting boundaries with a rageaholic you love might look like keeping yourself safe. While we can have compassion for their fits of uncontrollable anger, they do significant damage. Repairs are challenging, but not impossible. Without them the relationship becomes more insecure, and those in it feel under threat even when they are not. When rage turns violent and involves abuse, trust and bonds snap.

Rage traumatizes small children. Their systems cannot make sense of what is happening around them. Their safety and security are being threatened by someone they love, and who loves them. These children grow up to understand that this is what love looks like, and their systems become imprinted with stress and high levels of emotion around other's signs of big feelings. Cortisol is overproduced and adrenal fatigue affects them as adults.

If you suffer from bouts of rage, learn all you can about what is happening so you can work to heal yourself and preserve your relations. Seek out trained clinical professionals who can help you move it through your body, not management techniques, which call for more repressing of it. Rage has a way of finding a way out when not traced back to its origin and understood. Ragers need help so they can protect those they love and cherish.

SACRED NO

There will come a time when only "no" will do. It may be when you have become an expert at dishonoring your time and energy and processing healing or grief at a level where you have little time for others. It may be when you retire, after spending most of your adult life serving others. It might be when you decide to overhaul your life and create a new baseline from which to operate. It may be when the things you are reaching for no longer satisfy your deepest hungers.

NO is a beautiful word that creates a whole lot of YES once you've said it. It may seem negative, limiting, or pejorative, but used wisely it can be a gateway to freedom, preserving energy for the pursuits that are truly high-priority.

In the past, refusing a request might be taken as a great and rude offense. Perhaps it is because modern lifestyles have become so unmanageable that this is no longer the norm. Maybe we can see overwhelm in one another clearly enough to not lay claim lightly to another's time and energy. It is becoming more acceptable and essential to exercise our need to turn down even tempting offers. Thankfully, there seems to be a shift from imposing our needs on others to checking in. Our awareness is growing about how all of us are taking care of our time and energy.

It takes me three-to-four times the hours and energy to complete a project than I usually plan for. On this program, I am always running behind. In mid-life, I have wisely decided to wake up to how much it really requires of me to do a thing. I have had to disappoint others in order to honor what needs me most. A hidden benefit I wasn't expecting is that honoring my NO enables me to gracefully honor the NO of my loved ones.

EMPATHY NOT INVASION

I do not believe that it is ethical to feel someone else's feelings. This is a passion-inspiring, frequently discussed topic around the professional healer's campfire.

To a secure person, being "empathed on" feels invasive. To claim that we can feel other people's feelings is to entitle ourselves to their experiences in a way most of us do not appreciate.

Empaths and deep-feelers can identify with a wide range of emotions, making them valuable friends to have when understanding and empathy are needed. They can imagine, sometimes with great clarity, what others are going through. These are often the people we run to when we are seeking validation for what we're feeling, and some make mighty good healers. However, an empath wielding her shadow or ego can feel dangerous and risky.

If you know someone who is learning about their intuitive gifts as a highly sensitive person (HSP), discover whether they have the ego-strength to receive feedback about coming inside your bubble and laying claim to your feelings, if that is how it feels to you.

Everyone benefits from having energetic boundaries, and that includes those who feel very sensitive to what others are feeling. They may feel that they need protection more than anyone, especially if they are still learning to manage their own reserves.

If you identify with being strongly empathic, please tread with care for yourself, as well as those for whom you are "reading." Healthy feelers are needed, and it can be depleting when there are flimsy lines on both sides of this scenario.

MONEY MATTERS

We live in a culture and era controlled by economic policies, market stability, and employment eligibility. Few things have the power to scare us into "fight, flight or freeze" like feeling threatened because of money. Fears of economic collapse and unemployment rank high for people in all tax brackets.

We're not headed into less fearful times about meeting our basic needs for food, water, shelter, education, healthcare, and retirement. Current economic trends indicate costs rising while many households scramble to find ways to make ends meet and bring in more money.

Arguments about money are bound to happen in significant-other relations and among families. Secret spending, secret lending, impulse buying, and dishonesty about personal financial habits diminishes trust. Money issues can trigger extreme emotions and fears that require respectful communication to get to the other side. How we consume can also pose dilemmas.

What is the impact of financial stress on relationships? How often is it a reason for conflict? In the private spaces of our closest relationships, overwhelming money woes send stressed individuals into negative interaction cycles. Financial disharmony results in cranky emotions and careless treatment of one another while our minds reel. A partnership sometimes has to get inside one bubble with money, which means we need to agree on financial limits together.

It can be helpful to get money matters under control by creating reasonable budgets and shared documentation of spending habits. Sharing thoughts about finances when parties are not in a stressed or emotional state. It can be beneficial to come up with several ideas each, then sit down together outside the home to establish parameters and creative solutions.

Money conversations can be set up for success just as you would for any other intimate subject that triggers insecurity: lovingly, safely, and with a clear plan of what will work in mind.

BODY BOUNDARIES

Bodies are sacred and must not be touched without consent. This includes touching babies without parental permission. Not all pregnant women like to have their bellies touched. People who have experienced skin traumas, injuries, and physical abuses may not like to be touched. Anyone with fibromyalgia, rheumatoid arthritis, or inflammatory conditions may need to vary levels of touch. It's important to ask and create a culture where asking is the norm.

Ask before you hug someone upon meeting them. As variably social animals, some are more comfortable than others with physical closeness and contact. Try to recall the times when you would have preferred a handshake or a nod of acknowledgment. Under normal circumstances of conflict, hugs might feel welcome. In an inflamed or triggered situation, touch can feel invasive or hurtful. "May I give you a hug?" is called for when one person is soft and the other feels prickly.

I often hear adults telling children to give them a hug, which I find curious. We ask children to do things that violate their boundaries every day. We entitle ourselves to their personal space without consideration for who they are, and how they like to experience closeness. Embracing or laying a hand on a child's shoulder can be more about us than about them, rather than how they need or want to be handled. To sensory-affected and children with spectrum disorders, touch can feel alarming.

Consider asking a child if you can give them a hug and be open to the answer being no. An embrace is a gift we give someone else. Not all children or adults like to be hugged or fondled, particularly by strangers. We don't need to take it personally; what we need to do is honor what others want. Giving kids a choice in the matter will be carried through adolescence and into adulthood and help them do what it takes to protect their bodies by setting boundaries. Set the standard for yourself and for children that it is okay to create one's own signature gesture of love or greeting, and an entirely new chain of respect can begin.

SEXUAL BOUNDARIES

Children who are sexually violated are at great risk for developing emotional insecurity, an intense lack of trust, and relationship difficulty. This is completely within reason, and loved ones need to know that this is the case. Compassion must be given in the most difficult of situations. To be sexually mishandled at any age is to have your power taken away.

Imagine that for children, sexual inappropriateness of any kind is a setup for expecting more mishandlings and violations. The message is that our bodies are not our own, and we are commodities to be exploited by others.

As adults, reclaiming jurisdiction over one's body and sexual sensibilities is a heroic, healing journey. Beginning with boundaries among associates, friends, and colleagues, we can reestablish a code of conduct by knowing what we need and asking for what we want. Trust is developed through repetitive patterns and consistent respect of our personal space. We are unlikely to get this respect if we don't ask for it and do our part to cultivate it. This restores power to us. Gestures on our part to take care of ourselves gives the adult in us the opportunity to do what caregivers did not, or could not, when we were little.

With loved ones, we can establish even deeper trust by being open about our trauma, so they are clued in when we become triggered by what might otherwise feel like normal territory for one who has not had their sacred sexual nature taken advantage of.

Consider bringing your partner along to a therapy appointment or time with a healer, so that they can understand what it's like for you and helpful tools can be dispensed and mediated by a trusted party. They may not know that engaging in sex today can reignite the trauma on all levels. Hopefully they will be willing to take an active role in your healing and support your re-empowerment journey.

DIVORCE BOUNDARIES

Divorce is a territory packed with potential for the worst in a person to come forward. Unreconciled, unhealed shadows rear up and act out. Unmade improvements bring forth an attitude of apathy or resignation. Divorce requires the energy to persevere. Seek friends and counseling groups that can witness your feelings and help you keep your chin above water.

Half of all marriages in the U.S. end in divorce. Adults in the divorce process get to create a new model of cooperative structure when there are children involved.

Marriages that end in divorce are not all "failures." When two people have exhausted their options for healing the marriage—when they have shown up with the best they have to offer and cannot reconcile—it can feel like a terrible loss, and a failed attempt at good love. Divorcing parents must prepare for the stresses of child-rearing multiplying.

While challenging to manage the tidal waves of grief, priority focus must be given to children. Remember that what we experience in childhood is what we expect more of in the future. What level of respect can you and your partner rise into to model a fair and equitable separation? What might be possible if you can release the shame of failure? If you don't put your worth on trial, much can be eased. Honor the life you had with your ex and move forward, taking care that you are both fully available to any children you share, as they move through the stages of life without both parents in one home.

Boundaries inside of the divorce process might look like maintaining neutrality during exchanges and keeping communications to email so that you have the ability to edit and simplify. Consider hiring a mediator to help review financials and parenting plans, agreeing on the roles of future stepparents, and creating a contract for how new partners will be integrated and introduced to the children. Set up contact strategies in a way that minimizes triggers in the early phases.

Where there are broken hearts, deep healing is needed. Betrayals and wrongs that seem unmendable wear a person's spirit down. While you find your way, third-party helpers can assist with creating emotional security.

BOUNDARIES FOR CHILDREN

Unless children are taught about boundaries, they may not know that they get to have them. From birth, we parents are responsible for setting them up to be healthy and secure. We are entrusted with the job of showing them how they get to be treated. We model for them what asking for respectful treatment looks like, both with them directly and in the interactions they witness between us and others.

Beginning with setting feasible limits (no pulling the cat's tail, no kicking your siblings) when they are very little, we model that hurting is not okay. It doesn't work to set a double standard and hurt them to change a behavior—imagine how confusing that is! Too many interventions or unreasonable limits sets a child up for a fragmented attention span and a despondent relationship to their environment. If a toddler removes soil from a potted plant and is repeatedly in trouble for it, move the plant and other items out of sight so that the child can be free to live in the home. Set them up for success.

Many children experience the world through touching things and exploring three-dimensional shapes and textures. It's how they develop a relationship to the wondrous physical world they now live in. A pattern of "don't touch" creates frustration and burning curiosities, which eventually play out in a negative manner.

As children grow older, the rules change, and expectations rise. The very best way to teach about boundaries is to model them. If you don't want your child to invade the personal space of others, make sure their personal space is respected at home. Knock before entering their bedrooms. Ask before reading what they've written. Find out how the young people in your life want to be handled. Discover what they respond favorably to and imagine how your relationship with them will impact the security of their future expectations and relations.

INVASIONS OF PRIVACY

Boundaries around privacy are a national issue, family issue, and personal issue. Setting a precedent of entitled access to an individual's private thoughts can feel immensely violating. Where there are invasions of privacy, there will be diminished trust. Establishing trust seems to be one of the deciding factors in how we experience intimacy. Sneaky or secretive behavior doesn't build clean relations.

Think about the times when a privacy line was crossed. Was it when your records were revealed, your diary was read, your purse rifled through, or your phone records checked? If these things have happened, it is because someone did not trust you and wanted to find out whether their belief about you was true. It is not ethical to entitle ourselves to act as private detectives in order to find out information without someone's knowledge, and yet it happens.

Living in the technology age, privacy can be a matter of daily concern. When we have something to hide, why is that? When we don't want someone to know about a certain aspect of us, what is that about? Many individuals would refer to themselves as "private," meaning that they do not share what is meaningful to them, or their feelings with others, until deeper levels of trust have been established. Sometimes keeping information to yourself is not necessarily secretive, but a matter of personality.

We can navigate through privacy issues by asking ourselves why we are keeping ourselves from others, or why we want to know things about others that they would rather withhold. We can take responsibility for what is really at work. Are we afraid to make it known that we don't trust and want to know more? Are we concerned that if our loved ones know our secrets that we will be judged or misunderstood?

BOUNDARIES WITH PARENTS

Our first intimate relationships are with our parents or primary caregivers. Here is where we first experience true vulnerability. If our vulnerability was exploited, we may have developed coping mechanisms that now render us less willing to be vulnerable for fear of getting hurt again. These injuries can be long-lasting and impact some or all of our future relations.

Some adults find that they do not want to share the intimate details of their lives with their parents. Some parents of adults find that they are living out the consequences of long-ago broken trusts with their children. It is painful on both sides. Sound parents typically want nothing more than to have trust with their children throughout their lives. Different generations have various expectations, and children who do not "live up to" those expectations can end up feeling as though they live under a cloud of not-enoughness, or in their parents' shadows.

Relationships with parents can be difficult until old issues are resolved and healed, understanding expressed, resentments released, and emotional charges diffused. Bottled up hurts lurk under the surface, waiting to be triggered, and emerge at unexpected times.

When parents are not available or able to heal severe injuries with their adult children, it is common to establish distance from them. Forgiveness, mutual understanding and respect feels impossible. Boundaries might look like no-contact or low-contact rules. There can be conditions and terms by which the relationship operates under strained circumstances.

Adults get to make the rules about the relationships they are in and this includes with our parents. Being honest about what is needed from the parent, why the conditions exist, and how they might be improved in the future can help both parties establish a new model for conducting the relationship. Work with what you've got. If parent and child are of sound mind and open heart, even the gravest injuries can be healed and loved-through with dedication.

FAITH IN DARK PLACES

In the quiet places of the mind, doubts about our capabilities and what we're really made of lurk. Out in the world, we cope using the strategies we were given. We accommodate others' needs to keep the peace; we control the flow of the day to keep everything on track. We humans are quite good at keeping it together, until we find that we fear we cannot. Fear is responsible for dismantling security, and old wounds flare up when negative thoughts accumulate.

On a good day, while we are anchored in an authentic perception of reality, our higher reason guides. On a rough day, our minds drift like a lost helium balloon. The conflicts of the day spin a web of self-deprecating questions: What is real? What if my perception of how things have unfolded are off? What if I am to blame? What if I don't have what it takes? What if they find out I'm not who I say I am? What if I'm not who I think I am? What if the things I believe in are not valid?

What creeps in can feel like dark energy. While it's tempting to ignore the inner dialogue, it is beneficial to chat with it. Your consciousness requires protection from the crucifying stories that reside in the far subconscious realms. Your higher reasoning is the first line of defense against overwhelming tales of how it's all going to come crumbling down.

Creating boundaries with our own thinking process is a necessary part of being well. We can make a choice not to entertain the self-deprecating diatribes of the fear-mongering mind. These "gremlins" seldom make truly constructive arguments; their most valuable lesson lies in learning whether we are willing to make actual decisions based on their bad advice. Born of the shadows of childhood, they are the young, malnourished, neglected, distasteful prisoners. How can you re-parent the terrified parts of yourself into health by hearing what they have to say and comforting those fears?

FLIMSY BOUNDARIES

Why do I feel so unprotected? Loose boundaries come from not having your thoughts, feelings, and physical space honored in early development. As infants, we have few ways to communicate our discomfort. We now know that much more is contained in an infant than previous generations acknowledged. Rough handling, loud sounds, forced feeding, being handed off to untrustworthy strangers, and tickling (which produces laughter but can feel dominating to the one being tickled) can set a tone very early on that our space does not belong to us. The message in extreme is that we have no rights to our bodies, our privacy—we are merely the property (or the burden) of our caregivers.

Babies and children are considered sacred and holy in some cultures, but not so much here in the west. Overbearing parents who burst into rooms, scream and yell, dole out punishments, read diaries, and listen in on phone calls are a reflection of our national threats to privacy in the form of questionable Homeland Security tactics. When relations are secure, children and teens trust that they are safe to tell the truth. When dominated, they have nothing to lose.

It can be very hard to stand up for oneself, or believe that one even has the right to, when one has been overcontrolled and subjected to the overreactions of others. These behaviors create a pattern of withdrawing from communications or battling back in a survivalist manner. Those who have had their bodies violated have been shown that they cannot protect themselves, and that gaps in the protective field allow in trespassers. Those who have been mentally destabilized by someone they love struggle to intuit healthy choices and will invite more confusion into future relationships.

Healing the inner child's emotional, physical, sexual, and mental trauma can help someone who has no boundaries onto the path to being able to protect themselves. The first step is to seek understanding about what happened, and how it is playing out today.

SOMETHING DOESN'T FEEL RIGHT

Why do I have a nagging sense that something is amiss in my world? Our relationships can be the victims of inappropriate programming, but they also show us the conditions we're growing in.

It can be challenging to determine what is fear talking, and what is an intuitive or gut "hit" that is trying to guide us. The more healing we do, the more adept we become at assessing when we are truly in danger. It can be helpful to ask oneself, "What am I afraid will happen?" If the answers are extreme, consider asking trusted friends what they think. If you are not satisfied with their answers, seek a professional for consultation. Try to determine what the real risks are.

What we have available to work with is evidence. When a relationship doesn't feel safe, let's define what "safe" feels like to us. Is it a place where you can be honest and share your soul? Has this person ever given you reason to believe that they may not be trustworthy? Have they betrayed or compromised the safety of others? If so, what have they done to rehabilitate their patterns?

If you have been in an abusive relationship, elements of other relationships may remind you of the warnings you got when you were previously being exploited. It's a tough question whether the same is happening now, or likely to happen. Personal safety is of critical concern. If your personal safety is not in jeopardy, consider what it would take to calm your internal dialogue.

Have you considered what your loved one would need to do to put your mind at ease? How can you work together so that the relationship doesn't have to pay for the mistakes of others who have hurt you or confused your intuition?

GRIEVING THE LOST CHILD

It can be a challenge to be in relationship when you haven't grieved what has been lost. Broken innocence must be in some way honored and laid to rest.

Without rites of passage in modern culture, we lack ceremonious closure as we transition from one stage to the next. Losses of childhood feel like a part of us has been missing for a long time, and certain activities or creative pursuits may remind us that the child is still in there, seeking integration and acknowledgment.

Journaling and talking about what is affecting your heart can help you move forward into your future. When the past feels heavy and dark, seek to understand what is lingering in the dungeon of your soul that can be freed. If this seems complicated, a trained therapist or a neutral coach may be able to gently midwife you through this process. Do not be surprised if moving through a wound requires several years and much patience. Deep wounds take time to heal.

I have found that it sometimes takes a period of several years to move patiently through the deep woundings of childhood. There is something about seeing it through with love that helps to bind the medicine. I was taught to say, "I am in my healing process," when something from my past was affecting my external life and needed working-through. Relationships do not need to be ended or put on hold in order for this to take place. Life can continue on, but at perhaps a slower, more caring pace, which honors what you are going through.

To be in your healing process fully, let your loved ones know that part of your available energy is going toward a good cause. Make use of that time by caring deeply for yourself and seeking helpers and guides to facilitate your wellness.

SOUL RETRIEVAL

In transformative energy theory and practice, there is a healing treatment called soul retrieval. It can be quite useful for helping to visualize the fragmented parts of the soul, which went offline during traumatic times, come back, and re-join the spirit again for wholeness. A qualified medicine person journeys out into the soul realms to search for lost aspects and brings them back into the body. Sometimes this is performed by blowing the soul part back into the heart center.

Gentle and trustworthy guides can assist in this ethereal process. See Sandra Ingerman's book, *Soul Retrieval,* for a discussion on how this works. Her case studies may be able to tell you if this process is something to look into for yourself.

While you are in any healing process, it may be helpful to protect your energy by honoring it and giving yourself some time to grieve the losses and process them to the extent you can.

Entering into a healing process can feel quite vulnerable and leave gaps in the energy that act as open portals for hurts to come in. It is not that we are fragile at this time, so much as porous or fluid, like a river in which everything flows through us. Engaging your healing requires managing your energy. This is a form of protection in itself.

Protecting your energy might look like taking exquisite care of dietary needs, sleep requirements, and having a reasonable schedule that permits quiet time for meditation and reflection of what is moving through you. It might look like interacting more with those you trust and a little less with those you do not, until you feel strong again. The most important thing is to take responsibility for what you need because of what you are going through.

FALLOUT

When we begin to assert boundaries—determining our lines in the sand that help us and others feel safe in relationship—there can be casualties. Not everyone is keen to have healthy relationships if it means the status quo must change. Some folks are just fine doing life the way they always have. It may not be anxiety-inducing for them to live with unresolved conflicts or to sweep differences under the rug untended. They may not be accustomed to checking in with themselves about what feels right, and what is honoring of you or them. They may not be interested in deep, intimate connections where participants are free to practice self-care. An individual may have a number of reasons that do not allow for the kind of relationship you are seeking.

Boundaries are best set gently and with care, but sometimes they come across harshly. If you are new to taking care of yourself in this way, you might be surprised to find that setting up new systems of operation results in the temporary or permanent loss of friendships. When we declare to a person that the way we are being handled isn't working for us, they can feel wrong. The idea that they've made a mistake can trigger thoughts that they are somehow not good enough for us. This belief can tear apart trust. What helps is to communicate that every human makes mistakes, and it is okay. We make it okay by making new agreements that work and forgiving in order to move forward. It takes time to establish a new way.

In a relationship environment where no mistakes are allowed, or where improvements cannot be made without a great deal of hurt, egos are fragile, and the relationship itself is weak. It may not have the strength to survive the demands of wholeness and realness. Tender communication and a new ethic of allowing mistakes that do not threaten the foundation between two people is an exercise in bridge-building that fortifies our connections and leaves room for growth.

Love flourishes where there is room for humanness, imperfection, and forgiveness.

MAKE ROOM FOR HEALING

When healing the traumas and effects of childhood feels like sailing through dark waters at night with no lighthouse or shore in sight, hang in there. Take the time to clear your calendar of distractions and make a priority of being in your healing process.

When we enter into this space out of time, we are solo captains venturing into territory only we know the intricacies of. We can share what comes up with our closest people, healers, and allies, but ultimately it is a journey we take alone. It doesn't have to be an affirmation of loneliness. In fact, it can produce a knowledge that while our experiences are unique, many have taken the journey before us to find their serenity.

In our culture, it is common to medicate in order to hold the necessary journey at bay for as long as possible. While it may come knocking during our early adult years, we may spend the better part of our young adult lives working, becoming educated, having families, and following other pursuits.

I found in my late twenties that the knock at the door was growing unavoidable. The call to set things right in my spirit, body, and mind could no longer be ignored. I began taking meditation classes, shamanic training workshops, attending women's circles, and everything I could find to have assistance for what would come. A healing path became a big part of my life, and by the time my second child was born, I was well into my healing process and becoming less afraid of what the waters held, and that they would swallow me up.

This stage of entering the waters calls for bravery and support. Perhaps it will be helpful to write down your dreams and indulge the darkness of night as you begin to feel more at ease inside your skin—as you free yourself from the chains that have kept you from your most vital self.

FILLING UP WHEN DEPLETED

Building a solid eggshell takes from our personal reserve of resources. The needs of others are often tugging at us, as well as the general needs of life: to keep the cat's water bowl full, perform our duties at work, shuttle children to school, fix the plumbing, manage health issues, attend spiritual meetings or church, and take care of elders. As life force goes out, we find our energy spent. Then restore it with a good night's sleep and adequate nutrition.

When the rigors of relationship are trying, such as when we're attempting to find a wise way to do conflict and resolution, we may need some extra filling up. In the beginning of a new relationship, we're fueled by the raw hope and possibilities of new friendship. Even the obstacles are a joy to work through together. All is promising, and minor scrapes are soothed by the balm of closeness. As relationships mature, and we get older, the stuff of life piles up. The first glue breaks down and paying attention to what replenishes us and keeps us fueled for the journey becomes a more pressing need.

In the self-care movement, people are finding that moving their bodies, keeping energy and blood flowing, inspiring the mind with high-vibration music, films, and reading material, having meaningful conversations, spending time in nature, and engaging in spiritual pursuits are at the top of the list of resources for recharging.

What truly fills you up? Think of your day-to-day energy like a checking account. We have to make more deposits than withdrawals. What can you do for an hour or two that is a sure-fire way to keep you from drawing down on your energetic savings account reserved for true emergencies or retirement?

NON-NEGOTIABLE WORTHINESS

Our worth is not available for barter. We are human and of value in a way that cannot be measured in dollars, time, favors, casseroles, or shoulders to cry on. We are valuable because we are here. At any time, we can be a beneficial organism on the planet by honoring our lives as sacred.

Boundaries are a way to express our knowledge of our worth. They say, "My time and energy are needed here and there, but not well spent over there doing that. Endeavoring in that area does not yield qualitative results that make sense. Leave that to someone else."

It is not a determination of someone's worth, or lack of worth, that we find ourselves able or unable to be in relationship with them. Our involvement does not reveal their value. Some personalities and configurations simply do not work, and we do not have to exhaust ourselves trying.

When parents are faced with differences, they are wise, generous of spirit, and family-centric to try everything possible to work out their issues.

The trouble with feeling unworthy is that every gesture that travels out from it, no matter how well-disguised, will be contaminated with shame and the low vibrational quality that comes with it. Deeming ourselves undeserving of love, respect, and kindness is dishonoring of our existence and all that had to take place to bring us here—the spiritual details of which we can only guess. Thinking of others as "not worth my time" or "a waste of energy" is diminishing to their humanness.

In another relational constellation, an individual may shine brightly and prosper. Either way, it is up to each being to seek his own destiny. It is for us to move beyond our ego fragility and value everyone as equal in potential, with the ability to turn on a dime and change their lives at any time. We do not have to be near them or in relationship to hold this vision.

FOLLOW THROUGH

Discovering where you end and others begin is not about guilting, humbling, threatening, hurting, manipulating, or punishing them to achieve a desired outcome. Setting boundaries as self-care is different from self-preserving out of a lack of willingness to be vulnerable. When you find the line between how vulnerable you can and cannot be, you learn where your limits are. It can be tempting to withhold an offering of tenderness to avoid being hurt.

When a violation occurs, pain causes recoil. Take the time to determine what kinds of issues are deal-breakers, and which ones you can recover from. When we pull the trigger on setting limits too soon and out of fear, we may lose an opportunity to allow the relationship to stretch and grow. Drawing a line in the sand, and then erasing it, doesn't work very well. If it seems likely that you will come to trust again, give yourself time to deal with emotions before taking action.

Restoring trust involves calibrating yourself for wellness, moving through emotions, determining what the value of the exchange is, and taking it to a higher level from there. What might that look like?

To punish or banish a person in the name of boundaries practice would be to amputate the possibility for reconciliation. Revenge-seeking has no place here. It is a sign of emotional maturity to pause and ask what is motivating your choice and decide whether you intend to follow through. Threats to draw lines that do not play out result in a diminished quality of relationship and unnecessary stress.

Make choices that strengthen your spirit and your relations, not the temporary desire of ego.

DEVELOPING EGO STRENGTH

Building ego strength yields hearty individuals. People with ego strength are a joy to be in relationship with, because they have the uncanny ability to genuinely and gracefully hear feedback. Ego strength is not what it might sound like. It is not having an inflated sense of self or wearing a brave face to mask insecurities and fear. It is the cultivated skill of hearing before reacting with a willingness to think about what is being said, and how it will land. It allows us to hear the truth about how we're coming across in relationship and make adjustments accordingly when needed.

Our egos are responsible for leading us into the world in the form of self-esteem. This function helps you navigate your sense of self, and who you are in the world. When damaged and fragile, undermined and exploited, the ego will attempt to compensate for what it believes it lacks. The term egomaniac usually means someone who projects an image of themselves as superior in thought, skill, and deed, but it is rare that the individual believes this deep down. Boastful and self-important, egocentric qualities tend to push people away—the exact thing an insecure person does not want but is afraid to show.

We all suffer some level of insecurity. We can make repairs to our wounded egos by developing trust in our intuition, releasing the need for external validation, giving without expecting in return, cultivating relations with self-respecting comrades, and learning to listen for the truth in feedback without falling apart at the seams.

Practice by asking someone you consider to have fair communication skills to give you feedback about an area you feel fragile about, perhaps about the way you handled your child or how you come across when angry. Try to listen deeply and not turn up the defenses. How does it feel to hear about the areas you could stand to improve? What kind of feedback makes you feel like crying or causes you to have a negative internal dialogue? What is your process of discerning the truth?

Making a point to develop ego strength broadens our range for friendship, opens our ears to wisdom and changes everything.

AFTERWORD

When we are asserting our boundaries, either in face-to-face conflict or in written communication, there are many opportunities to create an unfair dialogue with the language we choose. To avoid projections, overexplaining, defensive responses (putting someone on the defensive), and an ongoing losing battle of which no good will come, choose language that supports your desired outcome.

Sometimes our egos like to go on a power trip and "get even" for the chaotic way we are feeling. We seek to shame, blame, diminish, demean, and destroy, like the goddess Kali on a destructive rampage. We may seek to put our heads in the sand, like Ostrich, or play dead like Opossum. These choices do not support our desired outcomes. So we may have to work backward. By envisioning the way we want things to turn out, we can shape our language with integrity and simple truths in order to reach a resolution and keep our side of the street clean.

In healthy relationships, a boundaries practice and clear language skills feel like self-care. They might feel like good, sturdy fences. You can still see over them. Energy can still pass through from a safe distance, but trespassing is not permitted.

The language prompts that follow this section can be read through with a bit of humor if you need it. Allow yourself to imagine how you would respond if someone said such a thing to you. Imagine how you would feel if you used them in a situation you are currently confronted with.

Which words and phrases feel organic and true to you? Which would feel awkward, but might be effective? The idea is to set yourself up for success, while taking responsibility. Try them on. Imagine yourself saying one and nothing more. What happens in that vacancy? The space that remains can be an uncomplicated, drama-free zone in which you refuse to drill the verbal dispute into the ground or sweep it into the shadows.

At our house where there are small children, we pass a talking stick (or rock) back and forth during a conflict, so no one tramples on another's words with interruptions and rudeness. It teaches respect and patience, and it allows everyone to become complete with their thoughts before moving on. This prevents shut-down and unwanted adaptations. Our jobs are to honor everyone's voices to completion in healthy relationship. If we can allow ourselves to become complete, transformation and wisdom can flow in. When you use a talking stick, you will come face-to-face many times with your own arrogance (impatience, frustration, demanding nature, eye-rolling, non-listening) in those uncomfortable moments when the person across from you is spilling what it is like for them in that moment. It's a nice space to breathe into, listen deeply, release judgment, and remember the sacredness, love, and respect you might be able to experience if you move past your own competing thoughts.

Have fun playing in the realm of new language and new possibility. Ultimately, it will have to feel really good, fair, and true to you in order to be effective.

LANGUAGE PROMPTS

I'm taking care of myself by _____.

I am choosing to step away from _____ so I can pour my energy into _____.

This is not a good fit for me.

I have the energy for _____.

I don't have the energy for _____.

_____ is leaving me depleted.

When you _____, I feel _____. (Stick to actual feelings: angry, fearful, sad, confused, happy—not projections, which usually begin with "I feel like you..." or claim a thought you're having as a "feeling.")

What I would like is _____.

What I'm needing more of is _____.

I feel understood when _____.

I shine when I'm supported this way: _____ (Be very specific and clear.)

I'm not okay with _____.

It hurts when _____.

I'm feeling triggered.

It's not a good time to talk about this.

I need quiet and clarity.

I need ten minutes to cool down. I need 24 hours. I need a week to become clear. I need a month.

Can I get back to you tomorrow?

I'll be able to give you an answer tomorrow.

I need some time to go into my heart and process this.

What if we [insert brilliant and well-thought-out suggestion]?

Let's put our heads together about this.

I need to create some sacred space around me.

I need to create some safety around my emotional process right now.

I'm freaking out. (This simple truth contains your own energy inside of your egg.)

I am taking responsibility for myself. My part. My actions. What I said that might have been confusing.

I'm wanting to operate at a high level of accountability.

What I'm hearing you say is: _____. Did I hear that right?

You seem _____ (sad, happy, confused, angry, frustrated, freaked out. Simple mirroring allows you not to take it on.)

I require total honesty.

I feel vulnerable.

I'm armoring up.

I don't want to lay the mortar while you place the bricks. Let's commit to staying soft.

In order to share myself with you, I require trust and safety. You can help create that environment for both of us by _____.

I can't hear you when you're yelling at me.

I shut down when you disrespect me.

In order to build trust, I need to give and receive respect.

This is where I end and you begin.

I could do that for you, but I'm wondering if it would steal your [lesson, medicine, teaching, wisdom] from you. (Especially helpful with teens.)

I'm able to trust when I have a lot of _____.

When you overreact, I shut down.

I can't make good decisions under this amount of emotional stress.

I go into a spin when you overcorrect me.

I'm feeling threatened.

My body is sacred.

When I feel disrespected, I retreat.

When I feel unsafe, I'm liable to shut down or run away.

I'm most likely to _____ if you rage on me.

My needs matter.

I determine my true needs by knowing who I am and being rigorously honest with myself.

I trust you to do what you need to do in order to take care of yourself.

I can't do any caretaking right now. Is that what you're needing from me?

How can I support both of us?

What can I do for you? I'd like to see if I can make it work.

I want intimacy with you.

I'm not able to be intimate with you at this time.

I can't allow myself to continue behaving this way.

I can't allow myself to be treated this way.

I'm feeling controlled.

I feel shadowy.

I'm wondering what's really coming up for you.

I can't do tantrums. When we can come back to a reasonable discussion, I'm all in.

I can hold a space for your anger, but I can't engage you in it. Do you want a witness?

I completely trust you to come up with a plan that will work for you.

Do you have some support around that?

I can refer you to someone who's great at these things.

I want to refer you to someone more capable than I am in this area.

This is what I'm willing to tolerate: _____.

This is what I'm not willing to tolerate: _____.

This is what will work for me: _____.

This is my bottom line: _____.

This is what it comes down to for me: _____ (make this a very clear and fair value).

I'm getting close to burning out and need to turn toward my [health, family, children, work, soul].

I made an error.

I misjudged.

Did I overstep your boundary? I'm sorry.

What are you needing most?

How can I be of service with the resources I have?

Does that sound fair to you?

Will that work?

How can we both feel empowered in this?

This is a total projection, so let me know if I'm out of line... (If you must project, frame it. Projections happen when we tell someone what they're doing or thinking.)

This is my thought about what's going on—let me know if I'm missing the mark.

I'm wondering if...

Maybe we can...

I'm having a thought... (as opposed to I'm feeling like...)

My intention is to respect us both.

No.

NO.

NO!

ACKNOWLEDGMENTS

This book would not have been possible without the encouragement of Melody Ross, and her habit of nudging me toward my edge. Thank you for believing that there was a much wider audience for these ideas and that I should stop what I was doing and get to it.

This book would not be what it is if not for the expert copy editing of Henry Cordes, superhero of concept clarification.

This book would not be in your hands if I was not supported at the spiritual, emotional, and household levels by Sky Sharp.

This book would be very different if not for the cheerleading and feedback from Jessica Knowles and the amazing women in recovery at Ramsey County Correctional Facility. Thank you for the hope and healing you bring, all of you.

This book would not have met its potential without the expert coaching in being a good ladyboss of Betsy Cordes. Thank you for showing me how to get it done in good form.

This book would not exist at all if not for the dedication of my layout and cover queens, Twozdai Hulse and Joanna Price, for holding me to deadlines, and for your devotion to this piece.

Thank you to Stephanie Anderson Ladd for teaching me the language of harmonious relations and how to get through my healing process.

Thank you to my guide, Mountain Lion, for inhabiting my dreams and journeys, showing me how to release my fears, and to the thousands of women who have taken Boundaries Boot Camp to learn about her medicine.

Thank you to Great Mystery for lighting up my heart with the inspiration to excavate my own terrain, swim my swamplands, and live to tell the tales.

Cherie Dawn Carr is the author of five books centered on self-healing through intimate relationship with the natural world. She is an enrolled member of the Choctaw Nation of Oklahoma. She writes as Lighthorse to honor the unheard voices of her ancestors.

Other Titles by Pixie Lighthorse

Goldmining the Shadows

Prayers of Honoring

Prayers of Honoring Voice

Prayers of Honoring Grief